EUROPEAN

DICTATORSHIPS

EUROPEAN DICTATORSHIPS

BY

COUNT CARLO SFORZA

FOREWORD BY
COLONEL EDWARD M. HOUSE

Essay Index Reprint Series

BOOKS FOR LIBRARIES PRESS, INC.
FREEPORT, NEW YORK

First Published 1931
Reprinted 1967

LIBRARY OF CONGRESS CATALOG CARD NUMBER:
67-26781

PRINTED IN THE UNITED STATES OF AMERICA

FOREWORD

To WRITE the Foreword to *European Dictatorships* is both a privilege and a duty — a privilege because it gives one some small share in the beneficent work which Count Sforza is doing toward the rehabilitation of orderly government in Europe — a duty because the world needs everyone's help at this critical hour.

In Count Sforza we find a man eminent in the affairs of his own country, refusing to let untoward circumstances deter him from seeking a broader field in which to offer his solution of the difficult problems which confront us all.

Usually books of this sort are written by theorists who have had no practical knowledge of the machinery of government. In this instance we have not only a student of world affairs, but one who has exercised his authority from one of the potent foreign offices of Europe, and in consequence knows the methods by which results are sought and achieved.

Count Sforza is a widely traveled man and has come in contact with the people of most countries, understanding their viewpoint and sympathizing with

v

it where possible. He knows his America as few foreigners do, and is able to touch on those matters which are of especial interest to us. He writes as a veteran, has a charming style, and his book will give pleasure as well as profit to those who are fortunate enough to read it.

EDWARD M. HOUSE

CONTENTS

CONTENTS

PREFACE

Before the War there was but one autocratic Government in Europe — the Russian Czardom. The German Empire itself, though ruled by strict military discipline, recognized the freedom of the Press, and actually, though hesitatingly, the Parliamentary system. Even in feudal Austria-Hungary, the local Diets secured a fair amount of secondary liberties.

It was only after the War that Europe was flooded by dictatorships which differed in their origins and in their ultimate aims, real or assumed, yet in one respect at least were all alike — in that the inner life of any country swayed by a dictatorship is solely ruled by a military, or a police despotism.

It was Cavour who once declared that any fool can govern by martial law. And martial law — made harder and more humiliating to bear when, as frequently occurs, it is not openly proclaimed — is the very basis of all dictatorships. Dictators know there is only one thing indispensable to them — in Russia it is the G.P.U., in Italy the Milizia, in Poland the Defensive; all of them terroristic organizations, hybrid instruments between the Army and the Secret Police.

It is not strange that most writers who have studied Post-War Dictatorships from a synthetic point of view — especially writers with democratic tendencies — should have confined themselves chiefly to this trait which all dictatorships have in common, and should not have brought forward the dissimilarities. While, on the other hand, the writers who admire or serve dictators usually prefer to advertise some special form of dictatorship, knowing only too well that their cause has nothing to gain by showing the links which unite the dictatorial landscape from Rome to Moscow, from Warsaw to Budapest.

Actually, when studying the origins of the different Dictatorships, one soon discovers how widely their initial historical characteristics diverge from one another; that even community of interests among privileged classes does not always play such a constant part therein, or, at any rate, so constantly preponderant a part as certain theoretical Socialist critics would have us think.

That is why it seems to me that there might be some scope for a book which would endeavor to find an answer to questions such as these:

Why has there been an epidemic of dictatorships in Europe since the War?

Is it a lasting trend, or simply a passing phenomenon of political neurasthenia?

What are the origins of the various dictatorships,

considered in the light of historical and social conditions which have produced them?

What features have the European dictatorships in common?

What differences exist between them?

Behind the deafening clamor that dictatorships — past masters, all, in the art of self-advertisement — oppose to the search of psychological reality, what can be the state of mind of the silenced masses?

I know quite well that it is easier to enunciate these, and analogous questions, than to answer them with full impartiality and critical serenity.

Nothing, indeed, is more difficult than to be serene on the subject of dictatorships. Supporters of autocracy, supporters of democracy, approve or condemn them according to the school of thought to which they belong. Moreover, dictatorships, like revolutions, are likely to cause reactions more important and more lasting than their immediate effects. No easy matter, therefore, to judge them synthetically until they have become part of the history of the Past.

But, if one allowed oneself to be too tightly curbed by these considerations, no history would ever be written, since so much of history is a continuous chain of effects and reactions. And an eye-witness has advantages which are wanting to the more remote historian; hence the interest which may attach itself to the former's remarks — and, as is frequently the

case in this book, to his own personal experiences —
on condition, of course, that he resists the temptation to over-systematize, modestly imparting to
his words the simple and honest value of testi-
mony.

Since an Introduction is the right and excusable
place, if any, for an author to speak of himself in
connection with his book, may I add the hope that
those failings with which my friends have often reproached me in the political field — to wit, an excess
of historical calm, and an inclination always to find
explanations equivalent to excuses for each event —
may prove not to *be* failings, in this matter of de-
scribing the troubling phenomena of Post-War dictatorships?

In order to retain for these pages the worth of personal witness — their sole value, probably — I have
refrained from giving to the ensuing chapters that systematic symmetry which a professional writer would
not have failed to adopt. The seeming advantage so
gained would, in reality, have been a pretentious
sham. What would, for instance, have been the use
of my adding some generic dozens of pages to the
already-existing plethora of books that treat of the
Soviet Dictatorship; or of establishing — from sec-
ond-hand information, since I did not chance to know
them personally — the characteristics of the already-
forgotten dictatorship of Primo de Rivera? I have

deemed it better, in the first instance, mainly to confine myself to studying certain special aspects of the Five Year Plan — that unconscious satire of the American Speed-Up System — as well as the continuity of an Imperialistic Russian policy in Asia, having watched both of them on the spot; while, in the second case, I have preferred to consider the psychology of one (a unique case among recent Dictatorships) who was the sole personal cause of the Spanish adventure — King Alfonso.

I do not need to sum up here the ideas which, even against my own will, have dogged me as I was summing up my impressions. Not to have concealed them, to admit that I remain loyal to them, is, in my opinion, an act of respect to my readers. I prefer humbly to confess, from these very first pages, that the more I have seen of dictatorships, the more I have felt what a terrible moral and material inheritance they will leave behind them; the more conscious I have become how precious was the phrase I heard from Samuel Gompers, the old American Labor Leader, during the Peace negotiations of 1919:

" Men do not know how safe a thing Freedom is."

One more remark I should like to add, for my American readers.

They should discard the half-pessimistic, half-complacent theory I have so often heard, from Iowa City to Boston — that an inevitable and cataclysmic decadence is occurring in the story of Continental Europe.

No; nothing too extraordinary is taking place; we are merely faced with a phase more or less recurrent, other parallels to which may be found in our common history on both sides of the Atlantic.

After the Napoleonic period, nations which had been bled white by twenty years of disturbances and wars, welcomed, or, more correctly speaking, seemed to welcome the stifling atmosphere of the Restoration imposed by the Holy Alliance.

After the World War, after the disillusionments of the Gospel of the Fourteen Points, after the excess of hopes raised by the Peace, more and more men in Europe, especially among the middle classes, began to think that politics had ceased to be true to their theoretical purpose of safeguarding the common interests. Hence a certain liking for the Mussolinis and Bethlens who had suppressed party politics in their own countries. The example and the fear of Bolshevism helped to strengthen such a feeling by adding to it the terror of the Russian vision, and the hope that so-called strong Governments might more fearlessly fight the Russian danger.

But has not the same phenomenon occurred even in America, though fortunate circumstances prevented the disease from assuming those blood-stained and brutal aspects which were seen in Europe?

The United States discovered, just as Europe did, that a war's worst period is the post-war period; as in Italy, in Germany, and — with more apparent decorum — in England and France, so 1919 and 1920 were, for America, the Zero hour of moral courage and intellectual faith.

Is it pardonable, in one who dearly treasures as delightful souvenirs his long visits to great American Universities in 1929 and 1931, to make no secret of his impression that many Americans, confronted with the phenomena of Dictatorships, should above all beware of the " Holier than thou " attitude?

The sufferings entailed by four years of war have sent great European nations stumbling into the pitfall of dictatorships. Granted. But if we get down to essentials, America underwent, morally speaking, the same phenomenon when, after some months of war, she slipped down from a Wilson to a Harding. Nevertheless, Americans were fortunate; laboring as they did just then under such depression and shock, they would have been quite capable of swallowing even a Dougherty.

But, after all, has it not ever been so, to a greater or lesser extent? After the heroic period of Washington — to quote America only — came Aaron Burr; after Lincoln, the carpet-baggers. . . .

I need not apologize to my American readers for drawing these analogies from periods of moral de-

pression in their history. I do it, not out of European
patriotism, or out of " Schadenfreude "; on the contrary: to draw, from these analogies, a reason for hope
and confidence in the future — moral forces never
lacking in America.

It was high time these studies were written; in a
few years no one will trouble any more about European dictatorships; at least, in the pathological form
they assumed after the World War.

EUROPEAN
DICTATORSHIPS

I

POST-WAR EUROPE
AND HER DICTATORSHIPS

DICTATORSHIPS we have always had with us; never, for the greater picturesqueness of history, have there been wanting ambitious men who sought to grasp personal power; that their numbers and their individual virulence should have increased after the terrible storm of the World War is not surprising.

Amid the political turmoils now disrupting European countries, and the lowering of intellectual standards (at once their cause and their effect), we too often forget that during the four gruesome years from 1914 to 1918 the flower of European youth fell — the most generous, the purest, the most ardent. What one of us, indeed, does not recall some friend who fell in the trenches, some bright youthful spirit of whom we had thought in the spring of 1914 that he was a hope or a sure promise for the scientific or moral life of tomorrow? When we wonder at the turn of events under our very eyes we are apt to forget

1

that those four years of war taught the survivors (or at least many of them) a vicious lesson: namely, that reckless violence was a duty; that blind obedience, even in matters of the spirit, was a national virtue. Military obedience, passive and immediate, was nothing, or almost nothing, compared to that wilful, stupefying submission to the falsest and most artificial theories prevailing in all the belligerent countries. These theories "patriotism" enjoined as gospel truths. Verily, were we to recall all this coldly, as if it were an episode of the Punic wars, we should have to conclude that the panic terror which swept over Europe on the eve of the year of grace 1000 A.D., that the fever which shook Europe with the first Crusade and its cry of *Dieu le veult!*, were but trifling episodes compared to the epidemic of intellectual degradation that raged throughout learned, sophisticated, twentieth-century Europe during the four years of the War and the anxious, troubled days following the peace treaties.

Beside psychological accidents so complex and so deep, even the dictatorial phenomena, be they violent but great as in Russia, or merely violent as in Italy, dwindle to very small proportions: like pustules on a sick body, they become mere external tokens of a disease far more significant than the pustules themselves.

The disturbing element in Europe owes nothing

either to the Stalins, Mussolinis or Pilsudskis, or to their would-be imitators in Germany, in Austria, in Spain, in Hungary and elsewhere. The significant symptom of the mental disease which has seized upon European thought is this: that there should have been for a time, not only " conservatives " who rejoiced in the destruction of laws — naïvely convinced that they were thus serving their immediate interests — but also intellectuals, sons of liberty, who failed to realize that, in vindicating régimes destructive of freedom, they thereby disavowed their own fundamental principles.

It is, moreover, worth noting that many of the writers (and not the least eminent, those who in recent years have professed their admiration for, or sympathy with, dictatorial régimes) are the very men who in pre-war Italy, Germany and France, were wont to proclaim the State, the Nation, as God. Underlying these movements of thought — and explaining them — three passions are found which certainly have existed for centuries, but which never, I believe, have so instinctively emerged side by side, barefaced, and with no attempt whatever at disguise of any sort, in Germany as in Italy, in France as in certain English circles which have not yet found their Mussolini or their Hitler, but are in search of him, as the Mosley movement sufficiently proves. These three passions are:

3

— the revanche *offensive of autocracies against democracies: a result mainly of the war habit;*

— the war waged by industrials and land-owners, soi-disant *against the Bolshevist danger, but in reality against any kind of socialist or labor movement: a result, for the greater part, of the fear of Russian Bolshevism (a fear that, in its most unreasoned form, constitutes one of the two main dangers of American and European civilization, the other being Bolshevism itself);*

— finally, although much less important, the anti-Semitic movement; which, under dictatorial management, has come to light even in countries where, like Italy, it had hitherto been unknown.

A certain dissatisfaction with parliamentary institutions in Europe did the rest. Leaving out of the question the Italian and Polish parliaments, which have remained in formal existence simply as decoys for foreign public opinion, there is no doubt that even in France and Great Britain parliamentary institutions are no longer regarded with the veneration and love which was their mainstay in our grandfathers' day. But it is wrong to identify parliamentary institutions with democracy. That the identification has been possible in the troubled years of the post-war period explains why even sensible people and good citizens have felt a tender spot for dictators and their gestures.

4

Even those — especially those, I should like to say — who, like myself, have kept entire faith in democracy and have felt from the very first hour how inadequate, childish and dangerous the dictatorial remedy was, must be ready to admit that a problem concerning parliaments does exist — or, to be more precise, we are faced with the problem of how to rationalize parliaments.

In the days of horses we could leave the roads to common sense. But the high speed automotive traffic of a modern street imposed dictatorial lights at the corners of American avenues, which were soon imitated in Europe.

An analogous change is occurring in every department of social life. Governments and parliaments are forced to concern themselves with a whole system of economic as well as political laws.

What everybody sees in parliaments I experienced, personally, in cabinets. According to a venerable custom, each minister had to bring to the cabinet meetings certain bills for our common approval before submitting them to parliament. But so numerous were these bills that the cabinet usually ended by taking a lively interest only in those having a political issue. This system still functions in France and Great Britain, with the result that each minister of the cabinet works only with his own subordinates without the collaboration of the rest of the ministers.

5

In a parliament the trouble is more evident: too many laws. The disorders of the parliamentary system are due not to bad personnel, but to conditions which would prevent the best conceivable personnel from acting as an efficient legislature.

The remedy offered by fascist régimes quickly proved to all honest minds a delusion. Dictators are obliged, for their own sake, to increase the centralization of power still further, which, in the long run, conduces to all the inconveniences of parliamentary régimes and none of their advantages. They have the same incompetence, the same decisions of anonymous administrations; but no longer do they have the criticism of public discussion, the only remedy existing against corruption.

The inconveniences of parliamentary life will probably be checked in the end through a remedy which will prove just as effective against the blind adventures of dictators: the remedy I am thinking of will consist of accepting, or pushing, the principle of federalism (or regionalism, as one might say for Italy and for France). Consider, for example, the British Parliament: the House of Commons ought to remain the supreme legislature; while questions relating to health, agriculture, mines, public works, etc., should be dealt with by local assemblies for England, Scotland and Wales. In consequence, the business of the House of Commons would be halved, with the result

6

that its functions of control of foreign, military and imperial affairs would be done efficiently instead of inefficiently, and the prestige of the Commons would rise again to the heights of the great English parliamentary epochs.[1]

But it was natural enough that dissatisfaction with parliament mingled with the tendencies and interests enumerated above should have merged into the new turbid torrent of dictatorial partisanship.

The same tendencies and interests have also been responsible for the fact that all dictatorships have taken on a violently nationalistic color. One must not abandon the idea of war, even after the terrible experience Europe has undergone. Of course, one must go on paying lip service to the idea that war is a disaster which should be avoided at all costs; and, indeed, one does not want war; but neither does one want war to recede too far, or become too unlikely; the idea remains, more or less avowedly, that fear of an always possible war helps to keep alive in the hearts of men those habits of hierarchy, of discipline, of service which — till war does come — seem fairly useful even in ordinary daily life.

Indeed, it is that fear, and that only, which can explain the strange attitude observed among sets imagining themselves " conservative " when preventive meas-

[1] I am thinking of a reform along analogous lines for the free Italy of tomorrow.

7

ures against war are mentioned. One feels they only approve with their lips; they do not want war, but neither do they want complete dissolution of those national hatreds and misunderstandings that tend to provoke war.

There is a final trait which completes the landscape of dictatorial Europe. The few years of Italian and Spanish dictatorship have revealed it to us with the irrefutable value of actual experience: I mean the failure of the experts.

If there is one field where experts should have worked wonders, it is that of material welfare. Now, the Fascist legend which clever propaganda kept alive for a long time, to wit, that the Mussolinian dictatorship had ensured to Italy an era of social and industrial happiness, has indeed proved itself a fiction. Facts have been stronger than bluff. Mussolini himself, in his Roman speeches of 1930 and 1931, was forced to admit defeat.

Why have there been so many disasters in Italy, most of them originating in Fascist blunders far antedating the economic crisis of over-production now prevailing practically everywhere? One may safely affirm the main cause to be: that dictatorships eliminate courageous servants, critical minds, the best brains.

As I am not concerned, since I resigned the very day the dictator came to power in my country and maintained my resignation despite his written requests to resume office, I may well add that it was clear to all impartial observers that under a dictatorship capable agents stood no chance unless they debased themselves by a simulated servility and never ventured frankly to disapprove policies they considered baneful.

It had been fashionable for years, here, there and everywhere in Europe, and even in America, to believe that democracy is a form of mob-rule; while dictatorship should be a government by the best. Once more, the contrary has proved true; dictatorship is organized mob-rule, and often it involves organized lynch laws. All dictators have proved to be demagogues; and would-be dictators, like Hitler, arch-demagogues. No Prime Minister in Europe has been as prodigal of ready-made catchpenny phrases as the two or three dictators actually in power in Europe.

When dictators appeal to the feelings of the masses, they most often appeal to base feelings — if only because they endeavor to awaken warlike sentiments, and paroxysms of boastful and pernicious jingoism. Dictatorships, indeed, can only prosper in an atmosphere of war; and if their foreign policy remains peaceful, it is only because they are restrained by international environments that, luckily, they are not strong enough or bold enough to disturb.

A unique characteristic of all post-war dictators — except the *bon enfant* Primo de Rivera, who was not a

9

product of the war — is, that they are condemned constantly to excite the nationalistic passions of their masses, Stalin himself with his internationalistic gospel being no exception.

And it is of this artificial stimulation of jingo nationalism and of the financial and economic disorder which their régimes, uncontrolled by parliament, inevitably bring in their train that dictators will die. It should not be forgotten that in former times all dictators, Bonaparte included, could maintain their power because the synthetic problems of the State were not very numerous. The poor " dictators " of today (if flattery has left them the slightest sense of humor) must sometimes be secretly mortified when they see themselves lauded every day in their papers as the responsible authors of all resolutions and gestures; whereas they are so occupied with the daily show and the struggle for maintenance of power that, under their rule, bureaucracy has waxed even more powerful than in the past when, at least, it was checked by the double control of cabinet ministers and parliaments.

II

THE ORIGINS OF FASCISM

Fascism has existed, and has been a living reality.

Those Socialists who find an interpretation for everything in the Marxian Scriptures, and have been willing to see in Fascism nothing but a set of tools organized to serve Capitalism, are but a renewed proof of the difficulty of getting an objective grasp on the innumerable expressions of human life and its mainsprings — when one is a prisoner to some absolute tenet like the Marxist formula.

Without meaning in the least to imply that the end of Fascism is near at hand — certain phenomena may appear long-lived to the impatience of politicians out of power, while they are very short for the unfolding of the history of a great nation — one can nevertheless hazard: that what is still going on under the name of Fascism has lost most of its psychological interest. A movement which has become an instrument in the hands of such a Police State as even Czarist Russia never saw can no longer give an impression of independent life.

11

But, whatever be the vitality still existing in Fascism, its inception remains well worth studying; how it came to arise in a great country the very breath of whose life seemed — and was — bound up with the liberal, democratic ideas that had stamped themselves on the soul of Italy through Mazzini and Cavour; how it was able to create a Government; and how it came to be reproduced and copied — as a party — in a second great country such as Germany.[1]

The general atmosphere of post-war Italy made possible the crystallization into Fascism of different and sometimes conflicting elements of discontent, moral and material; just as, a few years later, a more or less analogous phenomenon made the Hitlerian movement in Germany possible.

Before defining this atmosphere, and this crystallization, it is necessary to touch briefly on two previous occurrences which induced — particularly in middle-class youth — a state of mind explaining youth's belief in the capacity of the Fascist party — as seen by them — to provide a real solution and a remedy.

The first of these is the morbid literary mentality which had been brought into fashion by D'Annunzio.

The second is the irritation created in Italy by the disillusionments of peace — whether real or artificial does not matter — after four years of a terrible war.

D'Annunzio would very likely deny his blood-

[1] See Chapter IX.

12

brotherhood with Fascism. For, with all his admirable poetic gifts, it is impossible to conceive of him as sincerely wedded to an idea, even such an entirely external one as Fascism. He started his literary career by being a pagan, with Carducci. But Carducci, the poet of Liberal Italy of the nineteenth century, was imbued with the moral integrity of his generation. He had sung the greatness of Italy — Italy, daughter of Rome — ; which was the very reason, by the way, of his failing to attain the universality of Leopardi and Hugo. They are universal poets, because they blended in their poetry the most ardent love of their Italy, their France, with the universal aims of all poetry. Carducci narrowed his Italy somewhat, in confining her within a Roman atmosphere, just as another of the great Italian poets, Petrarch, had felt and done five centuries earlier. But if Carducci was sometimes narrow, he was never decadent. Decadent was D'Annunzio, the poet of the following generation; D'Annunzio, who continued the Roman exaltations of Carducci, but spiced them with a flavor of lust and sensuality taken from Nietzsche, apparently unable to see the loftier and more complex message of the German poet.

D'Annunzio has furthermore been, in all probability, the most typical and gifted specimen, at the close of the nineteenth and beginning of the twentieth centuries, of the poet to whom all ideas are mere pretexts and occasions for the marvellous exercise of

13

Caporetto — a resistance instinctively organized by a nation in arms even before their commander-in-chief, Cadorna, gave the order for it.

The influence of a poet and his gospel of pride, violence and sensuality, remarkable as it was, only influenced that portion of middle-class and lower middle-class youth, the mentality of whom (as frequently happens with the latin middle-classes) was essentially literary, when — even worse — it was not purely rhetorical. This kind of youth is the same everywhere in Europe; convinced, in France's natural claim to hegemonic position; in Germany, that moral loyalty only exists among Germans; in Italy, that the day of the Roman Empire was the one and only moment in history, and that modern Italy is its sole and exclusive heir.

But, after so much war-time suffering, the disillusions of the peace seemed to many more Italians to be a proof of artful ingratitude on the part of the Allies. What is more, they would have been right in so thinking, if the blind policy of Baron Sonnino had not assisted the Allies in ignoring Italy's true interests.

The conquest of Dalmatia, for instance, as it had been planned by Sonnino and his Nationalists was but a sign of weakness: a suspicious barbed-wire fence against our neighbors; while those who wanted — and tried after Sonnino's retirement — to throw open the doors of the East to Italian influence, were much

15

more convinced of Italian force and Italian superiority than Sonnino's followers. But Dalmatia was full of towns, monuments, memorials of all kinds that were relics of past Italian glory. What more natural than that an ill-informed public opinion, unaware of the fact that the vast majority of Dalmatians were Slavs and wanted to remain Slavs, should bear with difficulty the idea of failing to reconquer the ancient Venetian possessions? However much opposed I was to a sterile anti-Slav policy that would have deprived us of any international liberty, making us the heirs of that Austria we had destroyed — and therefore the heirs of all the anti-Austrian hatreds — I could not help resenting somewhat the advice of " breadth of vision " which came so often from Allies who would probably have been annexionists against their true interests, had they been faced with an analogous case. From my very feelings I guessed and understood the anger of many of my compatriots. . . .

The disillusions of the peace negotiations crystallized, indeed, into a sort of feeling, widespread among Italians, that their country had been bereft of the fruits of her victory. It was not strange that a nation, worn out by four years of terrible sufferings should lapse into a fit of xenophobia, which became a most favorable field for the culture of the Fascist bacillus; nor that the nation should not have perceived some excuse for the Allies' shortsighted selfishness in the

16

lack of statesmanship and imagination displayed by Sonnino. Not strange if the anger and discontent showed themselves particularly among the middle and lower classes which had lost so many thousands of their sons on the rocks of the Carso. Not strange — since none of the men in power told them at the time — that they failed to realize how nothing save a policy of generous friendship and understanding could ensure for us and for our children the only permanent fruits of victory. Not strange if the Italians of 1919 lost the possibly unique advantage bestowed by any victory — the subjective feeling of having won; they ought to have been told that the War which had cost them five hundred thousand dead had ended in the final destruction of their traditional enemy, the Hapsburg Monarchy; while France and Great Britain were far from having gained equal results. French and British advantages were precarious, whereas ours were permanent; and this became evident from the increased importance of Italy in international politics; which not even Fascist foreign policy, lacking any definite program, has since completely destroyed. However, and contrary to these facts, the Italian Government and its yellow press gave out that the victory had been " mutilated."

To this state of mind was added the intoxication of Fiume.

The Fiume expedition, conceived and prepared by

17

others, was only joined by D'Annunzio at the last moment.

To many Italians, irritated as they were by the difficulties which they attributed only to the blindness of the Allies, Fiume had become somewhat of a symbol of victory.

To D'Annunzio it became his tool; nay, more: his stage. In the same way as the most contradictory ideas of his generation had been marked by him and reduced to mere motives for his verse.

But the War had brought to the new generation — as to everyone in the world — a sort of intellectual setback. It is not to be wondered at, therefore, that the young ones, particularly those who had not known the realities of the War, were dazzled by the splendid coloring of the stage-setting, and mistook it for a patriotic epic.

In D'Annunzio's Fiume of 1919 and 1920 were concentrated in germ all those elements which, a little later, constituted the first phasis of Fascism: enthusiastic spirits who thought they were acting for their country's glory; and, with these, all the elements which always resort to noise and disorder — disorder camouflaged, this time under the cloak of patriotism.

There were seen, mobilized for the first time, the offspring of the lower middle classes who, later on, were to form the staff of the first Fascist groups: clerks, small professional men, and students who sus-

18

pected that their University courses, patched up during the feverish years of the War, would only make dry bones of them; young officers who, having entered the War as civilians, had got their commissions in the trenches and hated the thought of going back to their small bourgeois jobs, obscure and badly paid. . . . How could they be expected to become post-office clerks again, or teachers; bank clerks or shop assistants?

It was chiefly from among such as these that the personnel of the first Fascist bands was recruited, after the rehearsal of Fiume. The same thing, indeed, has happened elsewhere in Europe. One might even go so far as to say that it has ever been thus; the phenomenon of the *Demi-soldes* after the Napoleonic wars was nothing more; with this difference, that they worked for Liberal revolutions, as the historical movement required. The Revolutions of 1820 and 1821 in Spain were started by Italian, Polish, French officers of the " Grande Armée "; and remnants of these retired officers still played a part in the riper and more general movements of 1830 and 1831 in Belgium, Italy and Poland.

Fiume was not only the rehearsal of the Fascist mobilization. It was also the birthplace of the rhetorical style which later on, with Fascism, deluged Italy.

The dialogues — in would-be Greek tragedy vein

— between the Chief and the People on the Agora, afterwards exploited by Mussolini on Italy's public squares, were invented by D'Annunzio in Fiume:

— *Whose the Future?*
— *Ours.*
— *To whom Fiume, to whom Italy?*
— *To us, to us!*

It is all this bombastic style, all this raising-up of ghosts from Imperial Rome that, copied a few years later in Fascist Italy, made too many foreigners begin to doubt whether the Italy of Mazzini and Cavour had not been created in vain. . . .

They are wrong. Just as wrong were, in spite of appearances, the high-brow visitors to Papal Rome of a century ago when, finding there only masquerades and Arcady, they coined the definition of " Carnival nation."

A quarter of a century later, in 1848, Mazzini, Garibaldi and thousands of heroes with them, showed the world that Italy was not the " terra dei morti."

What has been will be again. Italy's history is made of falls and resurrections.

Bibliography

(The books and articles noted at the end of this chapter and of each of the following chapters are not intended to represent the usual facile list of more or less contradictory sources. They are only the texts from which I knew that I could safely draw certain data and facts; being certain of the authors' intellectual honesty, even when I did not happen to share all their views and inferences.)

Ferrero, G. — *Da Fiume a Roma.* — Milan, Athena, 1923.

Mowrer, E. A. — *Immortal Italy.* — New York, Appleton, 1922.

Salvemini, G. — *The Fascist Dictatorship in Italy.* — New York, Holt, 1927.

Sforza, Count C. — *Makers of Modern Europe.* — Indianapolis, Bobbs Merrill, 1930.

Trentin, S. — *L'Aventure Italienne.* — Paris, Presses Universitaires, 1928.

III

THE NATURE OF THE ITALIAN
DICTATORSHIP

On the 31st of October 1922, Mussolini tele-graphed to his Fascist lieutenants: " We must have discipline and respect for others, and in no case must we infringe on personal liberty."

Several times, on other occasions, in these, the first days of his régime, he repeated the same instructions.

I am convinced of his sincerity, at the time; or that, at least, he realized such caution was essential to the rôle of a statesman. It has been all but forgotten, for instance, that when taking over power immediately after the " March on Rome," he found his Cabinet as follows: ten non-Fascists and only four Fascists.

A month and a half later, November 16, at the re-opening of the Chamber, his tone had changed. — " I could make of this hall a bivouac for my men. . . . I could have formed a government exclusively com-posed of Fascists. . . ."

What had happened in the meanwhile? The most natural thing on earth. Everywhere Fascist violence had broken out once more. Drunk with a triumph, as easy as it was apparently complete, the heads of the Fascist bands everywhere sought to attain power — all the power; the Municipal administrations all of which were either Liberal, Catholic or Socialist, were replaced by Fascists; in the Provinces, Fascist chiefs reduced the Prefects to mere tools in their hands. . . . And Mussolini declared for violence in order to remain head of a party of violents.

The fusion of Fascists and Nationalists into one party, which was announced to the country on February 26, 1923, did not rest.

The Nationalists were few in number; they were still the tiny group which had been alone in declaring, in August 1914, that Italy ought to enter the war on the side of Germany and Austria, " because the nations of the Entente were doomed to defeat, being Democracies." Few in number, the Nationalists constituted a sort of cenacle of readerless writers; they had taken their theories from the classical authors of French and German Nationalisms, a little from Treitschke, much from Maurras. Such as they were, despite the fogginess and pretentiousness of their culture, they represented a valuable support to Mussolini; they supplied him with a " doctrine," with polemists, with literary, if second-rate, *habiletés*.

Before his understanding with them had been reached, he had tried for one with the " Popolari "

23

(Christian Democrats) and the Socialists. In any case, in a long conversation he had with me during the first days of November 1922, after my resignation from the Paris Embassy — in the course of which conversation he tried once more to induce me to walk in his ways — he assured me that his program was and would remain " a program of democracy."

Once his understanding with the Nationalists was reached, there was an end of Mussolini's wish to remain in power with the free consent of the governed; he fell into the easy pitfall of violent oppression of his opponents, and exploitation of the power confided to Fascists. The formula, " All the power for all the Fascists," made of them an army of occupation in a conquered land.

An end had come to the short honeymoon which Italian public opinion and Fascism had spent together.

I do not know whether that honeymoon is accepted by anti-Fascist writers, whose writings are subsequent to imprisonment and beatings by Fascist hands. But, from my personal experience, I am bound to admit that it existed; few men, indeed, have been surrounded by so predominant an atmosphere of well-wishing — whether the wishes were enthusiastic or resigned matters little — as that which Mussolini breathed at the beginning of his power. Those who, belonging to constitutional parties, declared at once, as I did, their invincible mistrust for the adventure have not forgotten the unasked for warnings of " prudence " they heard from their elders. . . .

The Conservatives looked to Mussolini for a strengthening of central authority. The *Popolari* banked on making him one of themselves, or at least neutralizing him, by means of their collaboration and support. Heads of industry and great landowners who had furnished the funds for his campaign, saw in him their liege man, for ever.

Many, even, of those who had recently suffered from Fascist violence hoped that the man would prove better than his followers, and that he would bring them to heel.

But this general atmosphere of benevolent expectancy presupposed one condition: that Mussolini was an independent man, not the mere tool of a faction.

A new Electoral Law (July 1923) sealed the fate of all possibility of a free atmosphere. Mussolini and his purveyors of formulae — the Nationalists — had grasped too clearly that the short trial-time granted by the Italian people had come to an end, and that in a free election they would be turned out of office.

Indeed, the new electoral law — passed by a terrorized Chamber with death in their hearts, letting themselves be swayed by the cowardly " fear of something worse " — ordained: — that, out of 535 seats, 356 be assigned to the list receiving throughout the country the majority of suffrages, and at least 25 per cent of votes; and that the remaining 179 seats be distributed among all the non-winning lists, in proportion to the number of votes recorded for them.

The elections took place on April 6, 1924. They turned out as might have been expected, at a time when the potential fear of the Fascist menace had made it possible for the Chamber, the year before, to vote an electoral law which was the death-warrant of a free Parliament.

The murder of Matteotti was the epilogue of this period.

On the evening of May 30, 1924, after having pronounced a speech of out-and-out opposition in the Chamber — a speech bare of any of those veils the bravest were already beginning to wrap around certain unsafe truths — he said with a smile to his friends:

— Now you may prepare my funeral oration.

On the 10th of June he was, in fact, killed by five Fascists; and his body buried in a wood a few miles out of Rome.

The tragedy of his death, the amnesty granted to the originators of the murder, the scandal of the murderers' own trial and their liberation two months after they had been sentenced; all this is on record and is part of Italian history.

I wish only to testify here to my last personal remembrances, slight though they may seem to those who did not live through the times I speak of. Four or five days before his death I met Matteotti in the Via del Tritone; we halted for some minutes; the words we exchanged might seem casual; but their deep meaning will never be erased from my mind.

He was sorrowful for the turn events were bound to take; even sadder for the future of the Socialist party to which he had devoted his life; — so, at least, it seemed to me as he frankly recalled some of our long arguments with one another in the lobbies of Parliament. Yet, in spite of all, he was glad also; glad as a man may be in the consciousness of duty done, with disregard for consequences. Surely the phrase he had used to his friends in the Chamber on that evening of May 30th — " Now you may prepare my funeral oration " — was still ringing in his mind, though he was too proud, too courageous to express it.

I watched him walk away and disappear in the human swarm of Via del Tritone, in bright sunshine, his youthful-looking head uncovered, as was his habit. . . .

When, later on, followed myself by a flock of spies, I went to see his widow in her police-ringed house, she told me:

— In the last months of his life he used constantly to say, showing me our children at play in the corner of the drawing-room: — "They must be taught to love; there is too much hate in the world."

This was the ascending purification of a soul preparing to give up life.

In putting him out of the way, a wise choice had been made. The mistake lay in thinking that his disappearance would not arouse too much feeling, for the very reason that he was respected, but not loved.

On the contrary, the Italian nation did not hesitate for one instant. All Italy grasped the truth, without need of proof positive. There was one of those deep waves of public opinion which, in a free country, would have swept away any government, instantly. Most of the leaders of the Opposition, contrary to the opinion of two or three, did not want to hurry on the crisis; they believed in developments slower and just as sure.

In a debate in the Senate, Mussolini knew how to sing small; expressing his horror of the crime and his own conversion to the use of strictly legal methods. He had previously given pledges — or what seemed pledges to those who were anxious to avoid a conflict; he had given up the Home Office to a Nationalist on whom both King and Pope thought they could depend; and consented to his Fascist Militia taking the oath of allegiance to the King, like the rest of the regular army.

Three Senators, Abbiate, Albertini and myself,

made speeches to prove the responsibility of the Government. I stated the dilemma: " Directly, or, at any rate, indirectly guilty "; and gave proof of this.

Hateful as self-quotations are, I think that I may be allowed to reproduce a few passages from my speech, if only as a token of what we felt at the time:

" A nation cannot give proof of greater weakness than by constantly asking itself the timid question: what will foreigners think? A great people must draw from its own moral conscience its own reason for judgment.

" Allow me to quote here the noble words which Matteotti addressed two months ago to his colleagues of the Brussels Socialist Conference: ' We do not want anything from our foreign comrades. Every people must conquer its own freedom; if it is not able to do so, it means that it is not worthy of it.'

" Do you not feel, my colleagues, here, in the words of this son of the same land as Battisti " — Matteotti originated from the Trentino — " a national pride all the nobler because not flaunted in demagogic rhetoric? The flame of patriotism is lit in the most diverse ways; nothing is more dangerous for the future destiny of a country than to believe that one can quicken that flame by external compulsion.

" To try — as did the Prime Minister — to find in other countries examples of other ferocious crimes, in order to quiet the commotion of Italian consciences, would be to indulge in the same bad habit of over-concern with foreign public opinion.

" A great country must know how to look reality in the face.

" And the reality is, that elsewhere there have been crimes of fanaticism, crimes of class-struggle, of race, of party; but here is a crime organized — while other crimes remain yet unpunished — by men established in the very center of the government, and by the supreme Leaders of a party that the Fascists' national theory asserts to be *one* with the sacred entity of the Country.

" A crime committed by men whose criminal activities deceived their Duce?

" Well; but then the head of the Government has committed the unpardonable fault of having been warned by many against them, and of having, in spite of that, tenaciously defended them, as he did in a speech a few months ago, when he mocked the idea of a good tyrant being surrounded by evil advisers. These are his very words: ' The alleged " evil counsellors " of the good tyrant are men who come to me every morning with their daily report, and with whom I share full responsibility.'

" Why, on the other hand, did he never take steps against the crimes which, with a frightful but natural crescendo due to their impunity, may irrevocably have led to the Matteotti tragedy?

30

" The remembrance of the slaughter of Sonzini and Scimula still makes people shudder; but the State intervened and the culprits were sentenced to heavy penalties. The hyenas of Empoli were arrested and given up to justice by a Liberal Government.

" But the Honorable Mr. Misuri had barely left the House of Parliament where he had been guilty of speaking his mind from the seat he occupied as representative of the people, when on the threshold of the Chamber he was knocked down.

" The Honorable Mr. Amendola was attacked and wounded in full daylight in the streets of Rome.

" The Honorable Mr. Forni was beaten almost to death while getting out of a train at the Milan station, before hundreds of people.

" The Honorable Mr. Gonzales was beaten and wounded at Genoa at an electoral meeting, together with the national hero Rossetti.

" Now look over the personal paper of the Premier, and for each of these crimes you will find, only words of excuse for the aggressors, and mockeries, insults, and fresh threats for the victims.

" These examples are remarkable because of the public character of the victims, but are not more serious than many others which took place in every corner of Italy, beginning with the murder of fourteen workers, taken from their houses in Turin and shot on the banks of the Po, while local authorities were ordered

31

to withdraw the patrols from the streets, for fear of intervention by some naïf and zealous gendarme. In every case, no one is aware that the authorities have made any serious investigation or inflicted any penalty.

" When, by chance, one culprit was arrested, the Fascist amnesty — which, to my mind, will remain a blot on the history of Italy — set him free.

" Lack of discussion is a sign of death in a great country. Machiavelli, on whom the present Premier once thought of writing a Doctorate thesis, said: ' Those who condemn divisions seem to me to condemn the very things which made Rome free and great.'

" The trouble is that Fascism is a state of mind, quite explicable in certain respects, but lacking a positive theory of thought, and likely therefore to subsist only in an atmosphere of undisputed prestige or terror. Fascism could fight many battles, but not one of intellectual criticism. And this, Gentlemen, has been the signal of Matteotti's death. He was the most ardent, the most passionate, the best-informed of opposers. He was suppressed: discussion was forbidden.

" The murderers and their instigators were mistaken only because, having perceived the silent passivity of the country confronted with many crimes, they thought that they could act with impunity even on this occasion. Instead, Italy awoke full of horror. And Matteotti dead, Gentlemen, is the victor."

Our words, though listened to in death-like silence, were in vain. The Senators gave 225 votes for the Government, and 18 only voted with Abbiate, Albertini and myself. Nothing, however, would be further from the truth than to imagine that only twenty-one Senators saw straight.

Nearly all knew what to make of it; a large number, in all good faith, calculated that to overthrow the Cabinet just then would entail plunging Italy into appalling disorders, for the Fascists would certainly have attempted Civil war. . . .

Despite Parliamentary votes, Mussolini for a long time felt his own weakness; for a long time he dared not take action against the Press, which was — with the exception of papers in his pay — entirely against him.

A true journalist, he could feel, however, where the danger lay. On July 10, 1924, he made the King sign a decree authorizing Prefects to confiscate at their own discretion all papers guilty of publishing " false or tendentious news."

In spite of the danger — and the real losses which they soon incurred (confiscation means much more than censorship; it entails loss of material, labor, and capital) — all the big newspapers finely remained in open opposition. The public demanded and read no others.

Confiscation and threats — legal and illegal — went on; but the Press held out.

At the reopening of the Chamber, the former Prime Ministers Giolitti, Orlando and Salandra joined their voices to the universal reprobation.

The Bench, in spite of a shameless pressure brought to bear upon it by the Government, had done their duty, or, at least, part of their duty. On December 4, 1924, after dramatic sessions when the chief witness called was Balbo, one of the " Quadrumviri " of the " March on Rome," and later Minister for Aviation, — the Tribunal of Rome acquitted the *Voce Repubblicana* (organ of the Republican Party), who had accused the said Balbo of instigating the murder of the Catholic priest, Minzoni, by Fascist agents at Argenta.

The irresistible pressure of public opinion was proved by the fact that Giunta, then Vice-President of the Chamber, later under-Secretary of State to the Presidency of the Council, had to resign the Vice-Presidency after being accused of an attempt on the Deputy Forni's life.

The *Mondo*, one of the most important Roman newspapers at the time, edited by A. Cianca, published on December 28, 1924, a terrible document, in which Cesare Rossi, former chief of Mussolini's press bureau, formally accused Mussolini of being the real and principal instigator of the Fascist crimes.

Mussolini, who had been so long undecided, now proceeded to take the counter-offensive; impelled to it, some say, by the threats of his lieutenants; or, possibly, convinced that he must stake all on one throw. The fact remains that, on January 3, 1925, in the Chamber, he crossed the Rubicon of fictitious law-abiding and declared that all the crimes which had been proved were " the result of a determined historical, political, and moral climate " and that he took full responsibility for them.

The speech closed with the following phrase: " Be assured that within 48 hours light will be thrown on the situation."

And it was.

How it was done, is typical of all that has been underhand and violent in the Fascist era.

In the first place, the speech was addressed to a Chamber containing nothing but Fascists, the Opposition having retired after Matteotti's murder; and, immediately after having thrown down the gage accepting Ministerial responsibility for so much bloodshed, Mussolini prudently closed Parliament, in order to prevent the Opposition from returning to the Chamber and taking up the challenge.

Next, he filled Rome and all the chief towns of Italy with fanatic gangs drawn from the Fascist underworld, the bed rock of crime and terrorism existing in all large cities. One who, like myself, saw Rome in those days, will never forget having seen what Paris must have been like in the time of the Terror.

For — and this might have been written at the head of this chapter, so essential is it to a right understanding of the Fascist phenomenon — the Fascist movement stands alone in history as one which, having real or apparent reactionary leanings, yet had the whole criminal element in the country on its side. It is undeniable that the cleanest and most idealistic revolutionary movements of the world — American and French at the end of the 18th century, French in 1830, Italian in 1831, all over Europe in 1848 — had in their ranks not only all the malcontents such as the Napoleonic *Demi-soldes*, but also all the stirred-up part of the populace which has nothing to lose and will lend a hand in any immediate cause of disorder — even when the goal of that cause is a higher order.

After January 1925, the crimes went on, but took another shape. The idea was to terrorize even passive opponents — so greatly did the Fascists fear an awakening of the country's conscience.

The list is a long one; first Amendola, the young Conservative Deputy, who had been one of the leaders of the battle against Mussolini and who had always hoped that the King would intervene; in July 1925, he was set upon at an Italian Spa, Montecatini, and died some months later after great sufferings caused by the blows inflicted on him.

Then, the days of October 1925, in Florence, when among those killed was Pilati, a former member of Parliament, who during the war had been severely wounded; and whose last words to his wife were — The Austrians had wounded me, Italians finished me. . . .

If I may venture to add incidents which in those days appeared almost trifling, I might quote that, on the same night, same hour, my country-house was burned and Benedetto Croce's library at Naples looted. The fact that the two occurrences, one in Northern Italy, and one in Southern Italy, happened at the same time warrants the belief that they took place with some high authorization. It is difficult to believe that Fascist groups would have dared to violate the house of the greatest living philosopher without being sure that it was safe to do so.

Various attempts against Mussolini — whether real or arranged — helped to impel Fascism down the now fatal slope of a more and more utter centralization of all the powers, a more and more complete suppression of any form of activity, even mental and moral activity, which did not allow itself to be included within the scope of new Fascist formulae.

A last attempt — concerning the authenticity of

which grave doubts exist — was made at Bologna on October 31, 1926.

There are two reasons for doubting the authenticity of this attempt. Mussolini was passing on one of his parades; there were crowds; a shot was fired; a lad of 17, member of the Fascist *Avanguardie,* was killed on the spot by a Fascist poniard, as being the author of the shot; it was never known who stabbed him; and no real trial was ever held. Besides, an hour after the " attempt," a fresh offensive of violence was opened all over Italy upon all opponents; a state of war was imposed on the country, and, five days later, a most complete law was promulgated, giving at last a legal form to such an oppression as Czarist Russia never witnessed. It is therefore not remarkable that the attempt should have been designated by the Italians in their whispers as " providential."

On November 25, 1926, was instituted the Special Tribunal for the Defense of the State. All political " crimes " were reserved to come before it; the judges were Fascist officers; the procedure followed was that of a state of war. We know the judgments passed by it; in May 1931, that on two men of admirable moral character, Rossi and Bauer, both well-known political and literary writers. Both were condemned to twenty years' imprisonment for having published political pamphlets on behalf of the movement " *Giustizia e Libertà* "; pamphlets which were abused by Communists as being documents in defense of the present social order. A short while before, in December 1930, Mario Vinciguerra, author of important books on Italian and English literature, one of the most exquisite moral types I have ever known, and Renzo Rendi, Literary Correspondent to the *New York Times*, were sentenced to 15 years' imprisonment. Pathetic and ironical at the same time in a State officially a Monarchy, their crime was to have written and distributed leaflets which advocated loyalty, on the part of anti-fascists, to the monarchical cause.[1]

[1] Here is a passage from one of the leaflets distributed by Vinciguerra and Rendi: "It would be madness to ignore the following facts: the Monarchy with the Army, and the Vatican with the 'Catholic Action,' are the two greatest forces that exist in Italy outside of Fascism: nobody questions the fact that the King and the Pope are, in their hearts, anti-Fascists. If, up to now, they have the one, suffered, and the other, exploited Fascism, for what has seemed to them (right or wrong it hardly matters) the good of the Monarchy and of the Church, it is now up to us to reverse that system of interests, fears, and hopes, that has so far determined their conduct. And no one can fail to see that this system of balances is already shifting of its own accord. The Crown, more and more scorned by the Dictatorship, is well aware that to continue in its submission would spell the complete dissolution of monarchical sentiment in Italy; nor can it trust Fascism, which always keeps in store, as in 1922, the Aosta threat, and the possibility of such *coups de scène* as the Balbo anti-royalist plot of 1926.

"The Pope, on the other hand, is in continuous conflict over the fundamental question of the education of the young. Moreover, the supposedly Catholic, but in reality anti-Christian character of Fascism, and its increasing claim to State-worship, are bound to clash more and more with the Church. The Pope well

39

But, besides these and many other known names, stand those of many hundreds of workmen and peasants, each sentenced to 15 or 20 years of prison. " Communists " they were called; but " Communist " in Fascist language generally means one who opposes Fascism. Up to May 31, 1931, the Special Tribunal has issued seven capital sentences, one to the *ergastolo* [2] and hundreds of other sentences totalling 4316 years of imprisonment shared among 1312 Italians.

What these sentences of the Special Tribunal mean is, without doubt, fear; fear which, under the guise of ringing phrases, is overwhelming the Heads of Fascism confronted by an Italy forcibly silenced but manifestly hostile.

They are all sentences *ad terrendum.*

The Fascist Revolution in Italy is a gigantic house

---

knows that Dictatorships are not eternal, and cannot help worrying about the state of the Lateran Treaty when Fascism falls. It is obvious that the only way to safeguard these treaties is to negotiate before it is too late with the possible successors of Fascism. Crown and Church are well aware of what dangers would menace them if they remained entirely alien to the breakdown of Fascism, no matter how near or remote that event might be."

Rendi is forty. Vinciguerra is forty-four. The latter's more important books are: *I Romantici, Preraffaellitismo Inglese,* (a book throwing fresh lights on Wilde and Tyrell), and *Introduction to Petrarch.* A mutual friend, an Englishman, who succeeded in seeing him in the prison house of Fossombrone, his rich, curly blond hair shaven and wearing a convict's dress covered with arrows, said of him, simply: " He looked like a prince in disguise."

[2] The *ergastolo* is solitary confinement for life.

of cards which may remain standing for any length of time, but may equally fall at any moment; and its builders live inside it with buoyant phrases on their lips but with quaking hearts.

I did not guess the full truth of my own words when, in the Senate on June 24, 1924, I said:

" Matteotti, dead, is the victor."

Bibliography

Ferrari, F. L. — *Le Régime fasciste italien.* — Paris, Spes, 1928.

Salvemini, G. — *The Fascist Dictatorship in Italy.* — New York, Holt, 1927.

Trentin, S. — *Les Transformations récentes du Droit Public Italien.* — Paris, Giard, 1929.

IV

THE LEGEND OF FASCISM SAVING
ITALY FROM BOLSHEVISM

$\mathbb{B}$UT, I know. . . .

Those days seem dead and gone when politics had a touch of idealism about them; the Romantic period when New York acclaimed Kossuth without the State Department being frightened by it; when London acclaimed Garibaldi; and thousands of Italians sacrificed life and property at the fiery call of Mazzini.

One hears it said, now:

— Have it as you please; but Italy was in mortal danger of falling into the abyss of Bolshevism; and thanks to Fascism. . . .

Against this fact — supposing it to be a fact — a good many people would count the lost freedom of a great nation, the blood of Matteotti, Amendola and a thousand others as being of little worth. . . .

This indeed has been the terrible punishment of those Fascists who thought sincerely of serving their country: that, in order to praise a régime and exalt a single individual, they have been obliged to throw

mud on their own nation, asserting — or at least
silently admitting — that Italians needed the Fascist
castor-oil to keep wise; and that they are so degraded
that they like to be bowed under the Fascist bludgeon,
— the one remedy good for them against the Bolshevik peril.

The chief argument brought forward as proof of
the necessity of the Fascist remedy is the " communist " occupation of the factories in 1920. That is why
I want to state here simply what I know about this
period.

In 1920 I was a member of the Cabinet in Italy.
What I am going to relate is merely what I said,
did and heard at the time. An evidence, nothing
more. I will leave the readers to draw their own
conclusions.

There is no doubt — I must begin by repeating —
that when the veteran Liberal statesman Giolitti came
for a last time to power in Italy (June 1920) with
myself as Foreign Minister, the situation was far from
being an easy one. It was a dangerous moment. A
moral crisis was grafting itself on the economic one,
both being the inevitable outcome of four years of a
terrible war. And it is always dangerous for a country when the two crises are contemporaneous.

While the economic crisis was only too natural in
a country relatively poor like Italy, the psychological discontent had peculiar causes, the most serious

43

being the fact that an important part of public opinion, misled by a press which had assumed the monopoly of a yellow patriotism, imagined that victory had been " mutilated " as I have explained in a previous chapter.[1]

Revolutionary propaganda took advantage of this condition of things to flaunt before the eyes of an irritated people the example of Russia — a myth and an ideal. To the Italian ex-service men, mostly peasants, who had been told in the trenches — by their officers and by the official propagandists — that after the victory they would have the millennium, the Russian example meant, not communism, but just the contrary — simply that the old serfs had won, each of them, a piece of land.

The policy the Allies were following towards Russia consisted in building a quarantine wall around her as around a plague center. And it was this blind policy which accomplished the rest; Bolshevik horrors, real as they were, were no longer believed among the masses.

When we came into power, I, for my part, quickly realized the danger and did my best to dispel it. In my first speech in Parliament as Foreign Minister I said:

" Monsieur Clémenceau's policy of the barbed wire around Russia has been morally useful to the Soviets,

[1] See Chapter II.

44

for it has furnished them with an alibi for the tremendous sufferings of the Russians."

A little while before I had contributed something — modest in appearance, but very useful. I had facilitated a visit of a group of Italian Labor leaders to Russia. They were honest men; they came back and told the workmen that life was horrible in Russia; and the workmen believed them.

When, in September 1920, the famous incident of the occupation of the factories took place, which is still quoted as the excuse for Fascism, it was indeed nothing more than the last flash of a fire which in reality was slowly dying out.

The truth about this episode which took place only in Northern Italy, may be briefly summed up as follows: some industrial leaders were planning a lockout as a consequence of an ordinary economic controversy; the leaders of the workmen thought that it would help them, and their prestige, to order the occupation of the factories, so that the Government would be obliged to interpose and get better terms for them; the echo of the Russian revolutionary formulae had of course an influence on the rash decision. But there is no doubt that, foolish as it was, it was — at least in the mind of the workmen's leaders — a tactical move to frighten the Government; nothing more. The movement lasted three weeks. It died from non-resistance. Giolitti had refused to leave his summer

residence at Bardonecchia in the Alps, and directed
the work of the government from there. At one time
he received a delegation of industrial leaders. One of
these, more insistent than the others, asked the Premier to bombard the workmen in the factories they
had occupied. Giolitti replied with his courteous,
ironic smile:

— Would you be willing for me to begin with the
bombardment of your own factory?

The man declined.

A few days later the occupation of the factories began to peter out. The workmen tried in vain to entice
engineers and managers to join them; they declined
the invitation. The workmen felt that they were help-
less, the old Italian common sense did the rest, and
liberty triumphed noiselessly over violence.

Giolitti faithfully describes this episode and the
reasons which prompted his conduct in the following
passage from his " Memoirs ":

" *I had, from the beginning, the clear and definite
conviction that experience would teach the workmen
that their aims could not possibly be achieved. This
episode was to me, under different shapes and conditions, an experience analogous to the general strike
of 1904, which had aroused so much terror and then
revealed its inanity. I was firmly convinced that the
conduct of the Government must be the same now as*

then. I therefore allowed the experience to go up to a certain point, in order to convince the workmen of the impossibility of their reaching their goal, so that the ringleaders might not throw back on others the responsibility for the failure."

If only to produce a piece of contemporary psychological evidence, I may state what my impressions were at the beginning of the occupation of the factories. I was with the other ministers in Rome; we met and declared our complete solidarity with Giolitti in what he would decide. But I felt it a duty to write to him:

"Strange as it may seem, may I write to you as Foreign Minister about what happens around you in Piedmont? It is generally believed that the Empire in Russia fell in 1917; this is an error; the death-hour of the Romanovs was struck in 1905, when the streets of St. Petersburg were stained with the blood of the workmen, shed by soldiers launched against the strikers. If we do the same here, we shall create a legend and a religion. We shall look like Conservatives and we shall be the destroyers of the Italian Liberal Monarchy. I feel sure that you agree with me; for my part, I should go against my conscience in taking the responsibility for any other policy."

Giolitti's silence proved to me that he viewed the situation in the same light as I did.

When he returned to Rome, a few days later, the situation had gone back to normal. I went, with many other ministers, to meet him at the Termini Station. The only allusion he made to my letter was to say, drawing me a little apart:

" *Well, does one offer to resign in such a hurry?* " (This was his ironical way of talking, which made him appear a cynic to so many people. He really wished me to see that my action had not displeased him.) " *Couldn't you have waited to find out what I really thought? I never for one instant doubted that forcible repression, with bloodshed, would sow seeds of disorder and hate.*"

In 1926, the British general strike, the way in which it was ended and petered out to a miserable end, reminded me singularly of this episode of the occupation of the factories in Lombardy and Piedmont.

At that time, in the autumn of 1920, the noisiest part of the Italian Socialist movement seemed to have reached the apex of success; more than 2000 municipal administrations were in Socialist hands — a fact which was far from satisfactory to the more thoughtful Socialist leaders, if only because of the excessive rapidity with which it had come about.

But the failure — and even more than the failure, the ridicule incurred by the unsuccessful occupation

— undermined all faith in the extremist leaders. Ranks and numbers remained, but confidence and enthusiasm were gone. This confidence undoubtedly would have subsisted if the traditional " rivers of blood " had been shed. Finally, in January 1921, at one of its periodical Congresses, the Socialist party split into two hostile factors: the Communists divided from the Socialists, forming an independent party of their own, bitterly adverse to the Socialists.

That meant to Giolitti the end of all peril from that quarter. This was what he had been waiting for, what he was counting on. I remember his saying so to me several times in the autumn of 1920; And this certainty was one of the reasons for his inactivity at the time of the invasion of the factories. It was his conviction that, however divided the Socialists might be, they would instantly reunite if violence were used against the workers. As it was, by his temporizing policy he induced many of the moderate leaders to contend persistently and successfully, though in secret, against the illusions which had prompted the more violent and childish to seize the factories.

Of course, timid spirits were still afraid; fear is a bad factor by which to judge serenely the signs of moral changes. I remember, for instance, Sir George Buchanan, the British Ambassador who had been appointed to Rome after his embassy to Petrograd during the war and the revolution; having witnessed the outburst of Bolshevism in Russia, he was scenting traces of it more or less everywhere. One day I came to see Giolitti while Buchanan was calling. I jokingly denounced his apprehensions to Giolitti who, looking out of a window, said:

" Do you see that olive tree, Sir George? You have never seen one in Russia, have you? Well, you will no more see Bolshevism in Italy than olive trees in Russia."

The year preceding the arrival of Fascism to power the morale of the Italian masses had improved as steadily as their economic condition. If in 1920 the strikes had numbered about 2000, these figures had come down to hardly 1000 in 1921, the number of strikers being just the same as in 1915, the year of Italy's entry into the war. In a word, the same curve of progress as in England and France, where the same epidemic of strikes and disorders had taken place, although — by a strange psychological phenomenon — everybody seems to have forgotten about these disorders, remembering only those which took place in Italy — thanks to Fascism, — an Italian might say.

Mussolini himself formally declared, one year after the occupation of the factories and fifteen months before the " March on Rome," that all revolutionary

50

danger was over, granted it had ever existed — of which I am not sure in the least. These are the very words he wrote in his paper, the *Popolo d'Italia*, on July 2, 1921: "To say that a Bolshevist danger still exists in Italy means taking base fears for reality. Bolshevism is overthrown."

It is perhaps because of hundreds of phrases like this one that in the Italian public libraries it is forbidden to ask for and to read the files of the *Popolo d'Italia*. For example, it is forgotten by almost everybody that during the occupation of the factories the same writer (who was already the leader of Fascism, and no longer the Revolutionary of old) wrote: "The workers must not surrender without obtaining guarantees." Luckily for the cause of order, his voice had no authority among the workers.

Another document by the same author is just as impossible to obtain today as the files of the *Popolo d'Italia*. It is the program he wrote in 1919 for the creation of his *fasci:* it is worth while to translate this document verbatim:

"*1. A National Constituent Assembly, as the Italian section of the International Constituent Assembly of peoples, to proceed to a radical transformation of the political and economic bases of community life.*

"*2. Proclamation of the Italian Republic. Decentralization of the executive power; autonomous ad-*

51

ministration of regions and communes by means of their own legislative organs. Sovereignty of the people, exercised through a universal, equal and direct franchise of citizens of both sexes, the people to reserve to themselves the initiative of referendum and veto.

" 3. Abolition of the Senate. Abolition of the political police. Magistrates elected independently of the executive power.

" 4. Abolition of all titles of nobility and of all orders of knighthood.

" 5. Abolition of compulsory service.

" 6. Liberty of opinion and of conscience, of religion, of associations, of the press.

" 7. An education system of schools, general and professional, open to all.

" 8. The maximum of attention to social hygiene.

" 9. Dissolution of industrial and financial limited companies. Suppression of every kind of speculation, of banks and stock exchanges.

" 10. Census and taxation of private wealth. Confiscation of unproductive revenue.

" 11. Prohibition of labor for children under sixteen years of age. Eight-hour day.

" 12. Reorganization of production on a cooperative basis and direct sharing of all the workers in the profits.

" 13. Abolition of secret diplomacy.

" 14. International policy opened to, and inspired by, the solidarity of peoples and their independence in a confederation of states."

This document is no longer that of a youthful Red, like the many which that Red wrote — but of a man who became Prime Minister of a great country, scarcely a couple of years after such a manifestation of political and economic originality as: " Abolition of titles of nobility," ranking with " Suppression of Banks and Stock Exchanges." . . .

To read it is, probably, to become imbued with doubt as to the salvage work of Fascism with regard to a Bolshevik menace in Italy: from which danger, if danger existed, it is obvious that Italy had already saved itself.

Bibliography

Giolitti, G. — *Memoirs of my Life.* — London, Chapman, 1923.

Sforza, Count C. — *Makers of Modern Europe.* — Indianapolis, Bobbs Merrill, 1930.

V

THE CONSEQUENCES OF THE
ITALIAN DICTATORSHIP

Other legends than that of the Bolshevik menace were also most carefully fostered by the agents of Fascist propaganda and blindly accepted by a public opinion beset by the Russian danger.

One of these legends was, that Italy had found herself in a serious state of economic break-down, in the years preceding the advent of Fascism to power.

It would be easy to give a quantity of proofs disposing of this assertion; with the help of statistics taken from official documents of the period — which, in those days, were models of veracity — and even from the Commercial Reports of the American Commercial Attachés. But this has been done before. Enough to state here the following facts. They will suffice:

— Inflation had been stopped after 1920.

— A slow but constantly progressive process of deflation had begun; and, in consequence, the value of the Italian lira was slowly but steadily going up.

In December 1920 one had to pay 28 lire for a dollar; in June 1922 the worth of the dollar had fallen to 19.7 lire.

In 1920 and 1921 the Giolitti Cabinet declined all the offers of huge loans American and British banks had made us immediately after the signing of the Treaty of Rapallo with Yugoslavia (November 1920); I remember the very words Giolitti used with me and with Peano, who was our colleague for the Treasury: " Such a policy would be easy and pleasant, but it would lead to disasters and would render useless the courage with which the tax-payers have accepted fresh burdens; we have no need of loans; we can manage for ourselves."

The same principles and the same policy were emphasized in July 1922 by Peano, then Minister for the Treasury in the Facta Cabinet, as he had been in 1920 and 1921 with Giolitti and me: " Offers of loans — Peano said to the Chamber — have been repeatedly made us by important English and American bankers. The Government has not found it necessary to accept these offers, so as not to burden our international balance of payments with new debts."

This will, I think, suffice to show that Italy, in those days, felt sure of her own financial and economic future.

The sole mistake made by the excellent Peano, and by Giolitti — as well as by myself and my other colleagues in our own province — lay in speaking quietly, without emphasis or dramatic gestures, without declaring at each turn that we were saving Italy and, most of all (which we really were doing), destroying the Bolshevist peril.

What, then, really did ail Italy? She was recovering from a terrible illness, the World War; an illness much more serious for her than for France or Great Britain, because her economic resources were so much leaner. The most characteristic symptoms of the sickness were, in Italy, the strikes; although there is a curious tendency to forget that the identical symptom appeared in the French and British patient; and, if in a lesser degree, that was merely because both the latter were more solidly built from the economic point of view.

It is this epidemic of strikes which is termed " Bolshevik Danger " by the Fascist quacks, who boast of having cured the sufferer and of having marvelously improved the economic and financial situation of Italy.

The real facts are much simpler: during the War, the Italian currency had been kept up by loans from the Allied Governments; at the conclusion of peace the Italian Government was suddenly thrown on its own resources; hence the necessity — in order to face the exceptionally heavy payments dependent on the War — of inflating the currency. Naturally, as a result of such an unavoidable inflation, the lira began to fall; in January 1919, two months after the Armistice, it still stood at 8 to the dollar; in December 1920, it had fallen to 28.

Prices having risen correspondingly, it became impossible for the workmen to live on their old wages, the purchasing power of which had been reduced to one-fifth. This is the main explanation of the Italian strikes of pre-Fascist memory. Bolshevism, Bolshevik agents, political immaturity of suffering masses lectured about a newly discovered Soviet paradise, were only secondary factors which account for nothing more than a certain disorder in some of the manifestations.

The legend of a desperate financial situation found by the Fascist Government at the end of 1922, was one of the most skillful inventions of Fascist propaganda. On it another long-lived legend was built: the balance of the budget suddenly realized through dictatorial authority.

The slogan is known: the Dictatorship found a deficit in the budget of fifteen billion lire in 1922; it was able to reduce it to no more than three billion lire in 1923; and it transferred the deficit into a surplus of two and two-tenths billion lire in 1926.

But the fact is that the deficit which Fascism had to meet in its first fiscal year, 1923, was not the deficit of 1922. What an incoming Cabinet inherits from

57

its predecessor is not the deficit of the preceding fiscal year, but the revenue and expenditure embodied in the budget of the current year. There may be a heavy deficit in a given fiscal year, while at the same time the government is taking measures which will in the following year result in a surplus. When the Fascists came into power, the deficit in the budget was no longer fifteen billion lire, but already had been reduced to three billion lire.

To understand how this was possible one must not forget that the enormous deficits in the years immediately following the War were due to the liquidation of the exceptional liabilities connected with the War. The hardest strain of war claims was felt in the years from 1919 to 1922. During those four years, sixty-nine billion lire of exceptional war expenses matured and were paid off. They fell from seven billion lire, in the fiscal year of 1922, to three billion lire, during the first Fascist fiscal year, 1923; to one and a half billions in 1924; to four hundred millions in 1925 and to one hundred millions in 1926. The further the War receded in the background, the more the expenses resulting from it decreased, and the deficits fell likewise. The Dictatorship had merely to wait for the passing of the years. It reaped in comfort where its predecessors had laboriously sown. Fascist propaganda took the deficit of fifteen billions in 1922; kept silent regarding the fact that this deficit had already

been reduced to three billions when the Fascists came
to power; compared the figures of 1922 with the figures of the succeeding years; and as a result it gave
Fascism the credit for this success.[1]

[1] The " cooking " of statistics and figures is a constant feature
of the Fascist Government, contrary to the honest tradition of the
Italian Liberal State. For instance:

On June 3, 1926, the Minister of Finance, Volpi, stated in the
Chamber that in the Budget of the current fiscal year there was
a surplus of 668 million lire by April 30; on June 11, in an official
letter to Mussolini, he announced that the surplus had risen to
1,200 millions; on July 18, in a speech at Bologna, he announced
that on June 30, the surplus had risen to 1,489 millions; on December 6, 1926, he reiterated that the surplus was 1,500 millions;
on December 10, in a speech to the Senate, he gave the surplus
as 2,268 millions, a new windfall of 800 millions. During the following months, *while large Italian loans were floated on the
American market,* this imposing surplus, "unprecedented in
Italian history," — as Volpi said — was hailed as a most striking
proof of the efficiency of the Fascist Dictatorship. But a year
later Professor Mortara, whose publications have an official authority, stated that the surplus amounted only to 568 millions,
(*Prospettive economiche,* 1928, pp. 465–6); the Fascist deputies
Olivetti, Mazzini and Tumidei, in their parliamentary reports on
the Budgets of 1925 and 1926–7 accepted the figure of 468 millions;
and the governmental records finally adopted the same figures
(*Annuario statistico italiano,* 1927, p. 308; *idem,* 1930, p. 197).
The curious fact is that even this figure was arrived at only by
ignoring the loans of $100,000,000 which Italy raised through
the Morgan bank in December 1925, i.e. during the fiscal year
in question.

Another example out of many, (less noxious because it did not,
like the 1926 speeches, result in heavy, unproductive foreign
loans): the Report for 1930 on the State Patrimony shows an
increase of 14 billion lire, for the value of " Scientific and Artistic
material." Here follow the two lines of the Report, stating the
wonderful increase:

The revaluation of the lira is another of the vaunted results attained by the Fascist Government.

The truth — which succeeding events have proved more and more — is, that this revaluation has been its worst blunder in the economic field.

While France stabilized her franc at 25 to the dollar, the Fascist Government fixed it at 19. All competent persons, including serious American bankers, warned the Fascist Government. In vain: the Head of the Italian régime, looking only for an ephemeral success of prestige, overlooked that to force up the value of the lira meant losing foreign markets for Italian exports. Thus Italian agricultural and industrial exports received a terrible blow abroad; unemployment resulted at home; while taxation was increased to an extent none had ever suspected to be possible.

Another achievement of Fascist policy, the prohibition of emigration, is worthy of record here. Although its consequences have been less disastrous, it originated in the same cause: a vain policy of prestige.

In 1926 the Fascist Government decided to forbid

"Account F. SCIENTIFIC AND ARTISTIC MATERIAL
At the end of June 1928, Million lire: 293;
At the end of June 1929, Million lire: 14,049."

How was such an increase reached? Simply by a new valuation of the pictures of the Italian galleries belonging to the State, and similar material. (Speech by Senator Federico Ricci in the Senate, Dec. 12, 1930.)

emigration. It was one of the periodic fits of Mussolini's war talk. To keep as many men as possible in
the country — would that not be food for thought
among the Powers which Fascist Italy seemed as if
intending to attack? Would they not offer colonies and
loans, to propitiate the menacing dictator? Such were
the schemes of the Fascist Machiavellis. All passports
were systematically refused. A first decree condemned
all men who attempted to leave the country clandes-
tinely in search of work to six months to two years'
imprisonment, while the militia had orders to fire at
all who attempted to cross the frontiers. A second
decree enacted that no one could emigrate for more
than three years and refused to allow wives, children
or parents to rejoin any emigrant. Any one who did
emigrate was treated as a traitor.

The results of this policy soon made themselves
felt. While in the three years 1924–26, 558,854 persons emigrated in search of work, in the three years
1927–29 only 259,784 persons emigrated. Thus some
200,000 Italians were forcibly prevented from earn-
ing abroad the bread they have been unable to earn in
Italy. The unemployment from which Italy suffers
today would have been infinitely less if Italians had
been allowed free emigration.

Although dear old ladies who still say: " But the
trains are running on time now," are becoming a sort

of paleolithic phenomenon, must an Italian, or any thinking person, come down to examining closely that remark, so childish and humiliating — humiliating for those who make it?

When Fascism came to power, the rolling stock and the road-beds had been repaired; the terrible damages brought on the Italian railways by four years of war had disappeared — the effect of some twenty months of hard work of the very able heads of the *Ferrovie dello Stato*. The trains had begun again to run on time, as they did before the war.

But the Fascists took the credit to themselves.

In spite of the legend, the recovery from the great trial of the war had already begun before Fascism came to power.

What has not been said by the propagandists of Fascism is the fact that the Fascist Government has concentrated all its improvements on the main lines, in order to impress foreign tourists. But if one leaves the great trains from Turin, Milan and Venice to Rome and Naples and takes the cross country lines, one discovers that, very often, the trains do not run on time.

Almost as foolish is another kindred war-cry of Fascist propaganda and of its voluntary and involuntary victims: the " drained swamp-lands."

The general survey of all lands to be reclaimed in

Italy which was made in 1882 recorded 1,839,411 hectares. At the end of 1922, 840,000 hectares, or nearly half of the total, already had been reclaimed, and work had been started on an important part of the remaining 999,000 hectares. Therefore, between 1922 and 1930 the Fascist Government has done nothing more in this field than the previous Liberal Government. It is true that in December 1928, a law was passed stating that all unreclaimed land should be reclaimed within fourteen years, but this law only became effective in 1929. Therefore it is evident that the Fascist boast of harvests reaped on lands that have been reclaimed by special Mussolinian merits has no foundation in fact.

But let us set aside details which will be remembered some day only as proofs of the desire certain foreign public opinions had to be lulled with vain tales. The ultimate test of all successes for a régime is to have its people satisfied and favorable. Has Fascism achieved this success? In an interview given to the *Daily Express* in January 1927, Mussolini asserted that no more than two thousand persons in Italy were hostile to Fascist rule among a population of 41,000,000. But in a speech of May 1927, he assured his followers that he was in a position to stamp down any attempt at resistance. " There are today in Italy," he stated in his speech, " 60,000 policemen,

20,000 police commissioners, 30,000 permanent militiamen, and 250,000 non-permanent militiamen; and these forces are equipped with 774 cars, 290 lorries, 198 motorcycles, 48 motor boats and 12,000 bicycles." A rather heavy display of force to keep down no more than two thousand political opponents.

The expenses for police services totaled 250,000,-000 lire in 1922 and rose to 1,400,000,000 lire, six times more, in 1928. A rather large expense to keep down two thousand opponents. In his speech of May 1927, Mussolini himself had to admit that the present generation of the Italian working people is an unconquerable one, and that he expected that a new generation will come to the front more fitted to absorb Fascist ideals.

Fascist violence has not rallied the masses to Fascism. Instead, it has exasperated them and created a general atmosphere favorable to Communist propaganda.

And not only among the masses.

What makes sorrowful food for thought to all Italians who care for their country's future, is to see that — while disgust with empty Fascist phraseology leads a great many young University students in the direction of Liberal culture — others (far too many of them) go towards Communism, either from impatience, from hatred of a society which has allowed *that* to happen, or from disgust with the slowness of a recovery distinguished only, as the Democratic opposition leaders admit, by a struggle of ideas. The frequent, almost daily, sentences passed on Communists [2] result, as might be expected, in impelling generous hearts of young students towards Communism.

It may be that timid and " right-thinking " persons, terrified by this current on which the papers are silent, but which is none the less felt, make up their minds to support the Fascist régime for fear of something worse.

But it is none the less true that those who say that Mussolini has checked the revolutionary peril in Italy, give the reverse of the truth. The Fascist Dictatorship, with the suppression of every political and personal liberty, has created a new revolutionary peril where none existed before the triumph of Fascism. One of the greatest responsibilities which the Fascist Dictatorship has assumed towards the Italian nation is this: by utterly demolishing all free and representative institutions it has blocked the way by which it might

[2] There can be no doubt that Fascist propaganda describes as " Communists " in its communiqués, the greater number of Italians who are arrested and condemned, and who are very often Liberals, Democrats, or very moderate Labor men. The reason for that is not hard to find.

But it is none the less true that the number of Communists who were practically non-existent at the time of the " Bolshevik Danger " in Italy, has very much increased after some years of Fascist rule.

be possible to face revolutionary situations without the dangers and the risks of open revolt.

The destruction of all free and representative institutions has already made it possible to lay down the germs of another form of struggle, which would have seemed inconceivable in free, tolerant Italy of yesterday: I mean the awakening of a strong anti-Vatican feeling as the result of the Lateran Treaties of February 1929.

While it is impossible to belittle the responsibility of Pius XI for what will probably remain one of the heaviest blunders of Vatican diplomacy, it cannot be denied that the party who most eagerly willed the treaties was Mussolini: Mussolini who led the Pope into temptation through formidable offers, Mussolini who wanted to peacock through the world with the Pope beside him as a moral patron.

That the treaties were willed by Mussolini, and by Mussolini alone, is sufficiently proved by the fact that during the first ten days of February 1929 all the American and European newspapers were discussing in long columns the forthcoming agreement, while no Italian paper said a word, or made an allusion to it.

Only those few Italians who were able to obtain foreign papers, read of the imminent treaties. Not until February 11, 1929, when they were actually signed, were the Italian papers permitted to inform 40 million

Italians of the fact. Needless to say that, while foreign papers freely pointed out what they considered to be some of the mutual advantages and disadvantages of the " conciliations," the Italian papers were allowed no more than enthusiastically to approve. " It was the will of God," Pius XI stated, in an interview which he gave on the 21st of the same month. Strange that the " Will of God " should have required the whole Italian press to be muzzled for months, while divine decisions were taking shape.

In February 1929 I was in America. When interviewed by New York papers, I merely said: " This so-called conciliation is the opening up of a question which had ceased to exist."

Events have moved quickly in the last three years. Pope Pius XI, a victim of his own blindness, but guilty of having rashly gone through all the negotiations without seriously consulting Cardinals and Bishops, as he should have done according to the traditions of the Church; a victim of the illusions with which he had lulled himself (did he not go so far as to say that this treaty with Mussolini was but the beginning of further developments?), realized — too late — that the true Conciliation had already been brought about by the wisdom and prudence of the Italian State after 1870, through the famous Law of Guarantees. It was the time when the Popes mildly protested, every two or three years, that the state of things created in Rome was not accepted by them; the Italian Government took care not to make any answer; then, on the next day — as on the previous — confidential agents from the Vatican came and saw Italian officials — and sometimes the Minister himself, as more than once happened to me — and quietly and successfully arranged all the questions which, now that a " conciliation " exists, are becoming elements of menace and blackmail.

In spite of the purely passive obedience which the lower clergy in Italy showed to the pro-Fascist orders of Pius XI, after February 1929; although those Bishops who have stood prudently aloof from Fascism outnumber those who — following papal instructions to the letter — have, at least in 1929 and 1930, identified themselves with it; yet it is to be feared that, when the Fascist scaffolding does one day collapse, the world will witness an anti-clerical reaction in Italy such as has never been seen. I say purposely that " it is to be feared," for even those who feel no link whatever with the Roman Church cannot but deplore — if they are good citizens and tolerant minds — that what might have been expected as a free evolution of spirits should degenerate into a string of Jacobin violences.

It will hardly be otherwise: for once Fascism is no more, most Fascists will become madly anti-Fascist; the worst-hated leaders will disappear; the highest traditional Power extant will, naturally, seem to be the Papacy; and the masses will accuse it of having been an accomplice to oppression and crimes.

Then as always when the masses are let loose after long years of silence, even good, honest country priests who — despite the phrases of Pius XI — have never ceased to loathe Fascism, will suffer for the blindness of their chief, for the false show of religion that Fascism put up, with chaplains for the Balillas and a Catholic phraseology dug out, without a particle of belief, from the stuffy armory of the Sainte-Alliance. . . .

Verily, no enemies of the Catholic Church ever laid the foundations of future violence in the religious world, as successfully as did the negotiators of the Lateran Treaties of 1929.

But, a great people has such a power of recuperation from economic disaster, and even from intestine struggles, that the worst consequences of the Fascist Dictatorship, in my opinion, will be another one: the moral lowering caused by a whole succession of years of stifling oppression, on every plane of life, intellectual and spiritual.

No dictatorship can exist without servility. The prostration of the mind before dogmas, beliefs, and so-called ideas or ideals, is more degrading in

Italy — as, by the way, in Russia also — than any old-time obeisance before an Asiatic despot of yore.

What makes the moral atmosphere of Italy worse, is a fact evident to me, but not easily seized by foreigners, nor sometimes even by Italians. However long the tale of violence, however intense the fear inspired by the sentences of the " Special Tribunal," the great mass of average Italians are not bringing themselves to admit that " it " can last.

Hence this paradox: that I could mention hundreds of families — for instance in Lombardy and in the old Duchies of Modena and Parma — whose grandfathers and great-grandfathers put up a daily resistance to the Austrian Government and its armies, risking life and possessions; because the Emperor of Austria was, in the forties, the most powerful monarch in Europe, they knew that long trials and sufferings were inevitable if they were to rid themselves of him and become a free nation.

To many of these men's grandsons and great-grandsons, life under Fascism is more intolerable than under Imperial Austria; but they cannot believe that " it " will go on. And in that case, why risk one's liberty to eliminate something which is bound to disappear?

Such a state of mind does exist; it may be that I have quoted it in order to explain a passivity which might be interpreted abroad in a sense painful to my Italian patriotism.

I must, however, admit that, even in this shape, and with this excuse, this passivity is bound to leave some moral trace behind it.

Eighteen years of corruption, and of bonapartist autocracy under the Second Empire, lowered, for a while, the moral character of the French; the German character certainly was not strengthened by the Bismarck and Hohenzollern autocracy; the Russians are paying the penalty for having endured for generations the Czarist oppression. . . .

Bibliography

King, Bolton. — *Fascism and Italy.* — London, Williams & Norgate, 1931.

71

VI

THE MAGYAR OLIGARCHY

LIBERAL newspapers and radical speakers frequently associate in their indictments the Italian and
the Hungarian dictatorships.

Nothing could be less accurate, especially as far
as historical origins are concerned.

Apart from the fact that, in Hungary, Bolshevism
actually existed with the régime of Béla Kun; while
Italy — as we have already seen — had only been
confronted with noisy disorders which no longer had
any dangerous meaning when Fascism appeared;
apart from this, what differentiates the Hungarian
Dictatorship from all others existing in Europe is, that
in Hungary we find the old, typical phenomenon of a
privileged class trying to protect its own interests,
devoid of any of the other artificial or transient
characteristics which are found in almost all other
dictatorships.

In fact, the history of old Hungary repeats itself,
with no new features.

In the whole course of their long and checkered

career, the Magyar aristocracy and gentry never felt
or realized that it might be expedient or wise to admit
ever so small an amount of social justice and political
equality, into the life of their State.

The Magyar " thousand-year-old " Constitution is
a stronghold of rules framed first against the Crown
and later on against the people. Its very conception
of the " Magyar nation " entirely excluded the com-
moners. " The people " — so ran the ancient *De-
cretum Tripartitum* — " includes the prelates, the
barons, and the other magnates, but not the common-
ers." Not until 1848 was serfdom abolished in Hungary; and even today, thousands of Magyar peasants
are practically not much more than the former
" serfs " on the vast estates belonging to a few magnates, who practically constitute all the landowners
of the whole of the rich Alföld plains.

The main reason for the ostracism and for the un-
assuaged hatred the Hungarian landowners felt and
showed towards one of themselves, Count Michael
Karolyi, is, that he proposed, when at the head of a
short-lived Provisional Government, after the Armistice, to expropriate those estates, and to divide a great
portion of them among the landless peasantry. Even
worse in their eyes was Karolyi's beginning with his
own estates, which — after he was elected President
of the Provisional Government — he offered to the
people as a preliminary to agricultural reform.

These are things which big landowners forgive even less easily than radical speeches.

To the subject Slav and Rumanian nationalities, the Hungary of these magnates was as intolerant, as the magnates themselves were cruel towards their own Magyar peasants.

It is typical of old aristocratic Hungary since the French Revolution, that she has always fought for her own freedom to the exclusion of the liberty of others. A savage, ultra-nationalist egotism, drawn probably from the Turanic traditions of their race, fills the hereditary leaders of the Arpad land. Once only, in the course of centuries, aristocratic Hungary declared for a policy of wide and generous federalism. This was in the fourteenth century, and under a French prince.

No doubt both in Italy and in France the Magyar Revolution of 1848 against Habsburg tyranny aroused an enthusiasm the echo of which made itself felt even in the United States.

Still, even then, one Liberal statesman saw the realities through the appearances; one, but the greatest of all, Cavour.

May I be allowed to quote a passage from a forgotten speech he delivered, in the Chamber of Deputies, on October 20, 1848 — a speech of rare courage, when one thinks that, at that time, all Italians idolized Kossuth, the leader of the Hungarian Revolution, and abominated Jellachich, the *Ban* of Croatia, who had given all the help in his power to the Austrian Emperor.

" I will not," said Cavour, " go into the details of the great struggle in which Magyars and Slavs are fiercely engaged. I will only remind the Chamber that the Magyars, noble and generous when they were protecting the rights of their nation against Imperial tyranny, have always shown themselves proud and overbearing towards the Slavs who inhabit Hungarian provinces.

" Be this as it may, I am not here to make an apologia for the Croats, or even of their valiant chief, the Ban Jellachich. I will only say that the banner unfurled by them is the Slav banner, and by no means, as has been supposed, a banner of reaction and despotism. Jellachich has made use of the Emperor's name, and thereby shown himself an astute politician. But that does not mean that his chief, not to say unique, aim, is other than the restoration of Slav nationality. . . ."

Letters from Cavour, of the same period, show that he was probably the only man of his time to perceive that the fight of the Slavs against aristocratic Hungary was not only a national struggle, but also a struggle for economic freedom.

Hungary of today — a Hungary whittled away by the Treaty of Trianon — might perhaps have spared herself some of the territorial losses inflicted on her after the war, if her big landowners could have realized, in their own interests, the wisdom of granting better economic and national conditions to their Slav subjects.

In 1919, Karolyi — and with him Jászi, who had taken on the difficult task, in the Provisional Government, of dealing with Magyar relations with other nationalities of St. Stephen's Crown — paid for the mistakes and egotism of their predecessors. If Jászi had been a Minister under Francis Joseph or Karl during the War, and had been allowed to realize his idea of a federal solution, there probably would not have been a disruption such as the Magyar witnessed after the War. . . . But, when Jászi began to attempt the impossible, it was too late.

When, on March 20, 1919, a representative of the Entente handed to Karolyi the note indicating the new frontiers of Hungary, who thereby lost more territory than a frank application of Wilson's Fourteen Points would have entailed, the Democratic Government was brought to an end. Next day, the Red Flag was hoisted over Budapest, and Béla Kun's Bolshevik régime began.

The Soviet leaders proved to be even weaker than those of the Liberal Revolution. Their leadership — the outcome of the patriotic despair of many, of the insane and criminal tendencies of a few, and the customary illusions of the masses — proved utterly unequal to the task of government. In a country where the grudge of peasants against landlords might easily have been exploited, the Budapest Bolsheviks were stupid enough to make themselves hated by the peasants who, in Russia, had been the greatest initial force in Lenin's hands.

When, in July 1919, the Rumanians attacked Béla Kun's régime, they attacked a dying thing. All the Soviet machinery was already on the point of collapse, in Budapest.

The main feature of the Magyar Government which succeeded the Bolsheviks was that it did, and still does, represent a mixture of the old feudal aristocracy who, under the Habsburgs had ruled the country alone, and of the old Hungarian gentry who, during the course of the 19th century, had lost their former influence and had been slowly reduced to supplying the Imperial-Royal Government with personnel for all sorts of civilian employments.

The collapse of the Habsburg Monarchy, the sad ending of Karolyi's government, the bloodstained parenthesis of the Béla Kun régime, served — each in its way — to give increased importance to the Magyar gentry. Hungarian Jews had previously found in semi-oriental Hungary, where all the nobles were so extravagant and feckless, an excellent field for their abilities. From their pariah situation before Hungary

77

became reconciled to Francis Joseph in 1867, they had progressed so far as to represent, at the outbreak of War, a new upper middle class; composed with the aristocratic magnates, they were now the Bank magnates. . . .

The destruction of the Austro-Hungarian army, the dwindling of old Hungary to a third of her original size, took away most of the gentry's livelihood. Thousands and thousands of them, mostly State officials — especially of petty rank — or employed on the vanished private Croatian and Translyvanian estates of the magnates, had nothing left to them but to fall, starving, on Budapest.

Driven by hunger, they flocked into counter-revolutionary organizations; deep-seated class instincts helping them to such a course.

Then a phenomenon happened not unlike the one which — as we have seen — occurred later on in Italy with the advent of Fascism — probably the only analogy which can be drawn between the two cases. The great landowners started the work of counter-revolution. The Jewish upper-bourgeoisie helped its organization with their money. And in the long run, the middle classes of the counter-revolution broke away from the hands of their patrons.

The middle classes had first asserted themselves through the blood-stained violence of their fight with Communists and Jews; a fight which was not remarkably gallant, considering that the first gentry groups which, with Horthy as leader, began to slay Jews and Socialists, did so from Szegedin, a town out of Béla Kun's reach, since it was garrisoned by French troops.

To drive back the wealthy Jews, after having accepted their help, was child's play; the Jews being politically insignificant in Hungary, despite their great financial importance.

More characteristic of the new developments of the situation were, how and why the gentry succeeded in usurping a kind of dictatorial power, robbing the great aristocratic landowners of a large part of their former influence. In the struggle against Communism, the peasants had chiefly organized under their own leaders. They had remained, as a class, self-conscious; they did not forget the agrarian reform, the realization of which had been dangled before them by the Karolyi Government. In order to win them over completely to the counter-revolution their leaders were obliged to promise them, in turn, far-reaching land reforms. After the counter-revolutionary victory, the peasants represented a well-organized class, which the great landlords would have been glad to break up. To face this fresh danger, the aristocracy, despite its pride, felt that it must conciliate the counter-revolutionary gentry.

The latter were numerous, and could form a good

army. Also, on account of the relatively high standard of its education, the gentry was capable of a sturdier organization, and could carry on a more systematic and efficient propaganda than the peasants could.

Only one circumstance was unfavorable to the aristocracy; it could not well conceal from the leaders of the counter-revolutionary middle class that, without their help, the magnates' estates would be exposed to new attacks, and this time not from Bolsheviks, but from the peasants. Making the most of this circumstance, the gentry succeeded in seizing, in the midst of the counter-revolution, a leadership which was marked by barbarous mass-murders. After the victory, which they felt was *their* victory, the gentry — the middle class — took upon themselves to rule their country, since they, and not the magnates, had " saved " it, as they said.

Admiral Horthy, Regent of the Kingdom of Hungary, is today the representative leader of this gentry; one of themselves, he is a Calvinist, whereas most of the great aristocrats had remained or became Catholics; a naval officer who undoubtedly did his duty in the War, a shrewd fellow who knows how to advance his own personal interests without apparent disloyalty to his old Habsburg oaths, he puts one in mind of Bismarck's definition of the Hungarians: " Half hussars, half lawyers."

The Regent, symbol and chief of this new class dictatorship now ruling Hungary, was elected for an undeterminate period — a sure proof whence the *coup d'état* of the new régime originated.

A legal screen for the Dictatorship is afforded by the fact that the Sovereignty of the State is maintained in the symbol of St. Stephen's crown; a symbol indispensable, by the bye, to a real or feigned policy of continuing the historical integrity of the Kingdom as represented by the Crown.

The National Assembly of 1920 — imposed by the Entente Powers who wished the Treaty of Peace to be approved by a democratic body — was elected on the basis of universal and secret suffrage.

Since then Count Bethlen, Prime Minister of Hungary, has — first by an ordinance in 1922, then by a law in 1925 — reduced the right of suffrage so that, now, the number of voters is 25 per cent less than in 1920; and open ballot has been re-established, except in a few town constituencies; so that today, out of the 245 deputies, 46 only are elected by secret ballot, the only sincere form of vote.

This did not suffice.

It was decided that, to stand as a candidate, a certificate of recommendation signed by 10 per cent of the electors, must be produced. In view of the official pressure brought to bear on the electors by tax-collectors, by threats of dismissal, etc., even a party endowed with ordinary resources finds it difficult to assemble the requisite number of signatures. Moreover, the validity and authenticity of these signatures is scrutinized by an official committee, from whose decision there is no appeal. Thus, out of 2000 signatures, for instance, presented by the Opposition, several hundreds are declared invalid, so that ten to fifteen of the necessary signatures are always wanting.

Before the war in Hungary, its counties and municipalities possessed sufficient autonomy, even though based on an extremely restricted suffrage. As the county was the stronghold of the gentry, and as self-administration was a, at least, nominal, weapon against the power of the Habsburg monarch, the dictatorship has not ventured to destroy municipal self-government formally; but, in reality, it has been suppressed by a law of 1929 in provincial municipalities; and, by a law of 1930, in the capital, Budapest; local self-government has, in effect, been ceded to the central government.

Practically, we may conclude, all provincial and municipal autonomy has been suppressed in Hungary.

In order to appreciate properly the importance of the administrative organization having all passed to the direct service of the dictatorship, it is enough to add that the whole administrative machine still is based on the exceptional decrees issued during the war. The consequence is that, though there is no official press censorship, yet no paper can be published without permission of the authorities; any paper may be suspended by ministerial decision; the street-selling of newspapers is equally subject to an old war law. The press, in a word, exists in an atmosphere of constant apprehension; and all the newspapers have become flexible instruments in the hands of the government — although in a less evident form than in Italy.

No association can be constituted without the government's previous assent; which is never granted when even a few among those who might become members of the new association are not considered safe friends of the dictatorship.

Impossible, therefore, to have a public opinion in Hungary. All that might form it, and promote it, is kept in the hands of the dictatorship.

As for the administration of justice, enough to quote Article 7 of the law of 1921, for the " Protection of Public and Social Order ":

" Whoever shall state or repeat an untruth affecting the good name of the Hungarian State or the Hungarian Nation shall be liable to a term of imprisonment not exceeding five years."

A list of recent judgments goes to prove that even an affirmation of true facts may be punishable, since — to quote one judgment out of a hundred — " through the arrangement and generalization of facts which were true, a false account of public affairs has been created."

Thus, a Hungarian, or a foreigner in Hungary who would dare to say that a prince Windischgrätz had been forging French banknotes, that these notes had been printed by the official Cartographical Institute, and that the Hungarian Foreign Office had passed them over into Holland to be spent there, would be telling a series of absolute truths; but, legally, these truths would send him to spend five years in prison.

Such laws as these weigh down a country with a silence of death.

Moreover, should anyone wish to speak up, an unwritten inevitable penalty — apart from that provided under Article 7 of the law of 1921 — could at any moment touch him in his financial interests, whether great or small; for a series of decrees has put all economic activities under State control; therefore no landowner who ventured to speak against the Government could obtain a loan or mortgage; no lawyer who was really anti-Government would keep his clients; no architect who was not " right-thinking " would get commissions; no " red " dancing teacher would find pupils. . . .

A certain outward show of decorum is maintained in the Hungarian Parliament, more skillfully than in Italy; but its independence is equally nil. We must not forget that in the National Assembly which preceded the present Chamber of Deputies, the majority consisted of small landowners. It has since been possible for Count Bethlen, thanks to the electoral system I have explained, to remove all hostile elements, reducing the number of small landowners to an infinitesimal figure. Even the selection of Opposition members is, to a certain extent, in the hands of the Dictatorship.

Let us sum up.

First of all, we must admit that, despite Horthy's original *coup*, and despite the power possessed by the Prime Minister Count Bethlen, the Hungarian Dictatorship is not, as in Italy, a personal one.

Neither is it, in spite of its origin, a military one, as in Poland. This is because the Hungarian nobility — be they magnates or gentry — made it a point of pride, all through the Habsburg domination, to ignore the army. The army was "*Kaiserlich*"; to ignore it was to be a good Magyar patriot. No doubt, the present Hungarian army is strongly for the Dictatorship, and is in close touch with the officers who surround Horthy. But it does not form an integral part of the Hungarian oligarchy.

What composes and makes the strength of the Magyar oligarchy is:

— The members of the aristocracy who are not Legitimists. (The Legitimists, however, while hating to see power entirely in the hands of a man of small nobility, such as Horthy, and while retaining a theoretical loyalty to the son of the last Emperor — King Karl — take good care not to fight the present régime, except with *salon* words; they know that they depend on it for too many daily favors; and they find that a simple policy of sulks has the double advantage of demonstrating their Habsburg loyalty, and of gathering more advantages from the present Government.)

— The Catholic clergy, whose influence is enhanced — paradoxic as it may seem — by the fact that both Horthy and Bethlen are Calvinists.

— The higher officials of State bureaucracy.

— And, last but not least, the more pushing, intelligent of the gentry, who know that the present régime is really *theirs*, and that it may bring them advantages and advancement undreamed of under former Governments.

The Cabinet is at once the expression, and an integral part, of the oligarchy.

We have seen that the oligarchy and its government have in their hands all possible means of domination. One detail, usually ignored abroad, will serve still further to show their strength: the noisy Fascist groups of the " Awakening Magyars," which were formerly so much to the front, have, little by little, skillfully but relentlessly, been divested of all importance by the Government. After being, at one time, the chief instrument of the Hungarian Terror, the

" Awakening Magyars " today are only used by the Government as scarecrows to frighten the countries of the Little Entente, especially Jugoslavia.

One may add that even the scanty existing groups of Opposition — either Socialist-Democrats, Democrats or Liberals — practically are in the service of the Magyar regime. They are so, because with their mild Opposition speeches (which are mild perforce) they supply the necessary Parliamentary make-up to deceive foreign public opinion; because — through the silence with which they veil facts and injustices far more serious than the trifles they denounce — they mislead those who, abroad, take their criticisms seriously.

The dictatorship of the Magyar oligarchy is without comparison stronger and stabler than the Italian. Horthy and Bethlen have not to fear nor to fight, as their congeners in Italy must do, either the *bourgeoisie* (which never existed in Hungary in the Western sense of the word), nor yet a class of workmen taught by years of free labor propaganda to feel classconscious of its own rights and interests; not to mention the fact that Hungarian workmen are still paying the penalty for their foolish co-operation, in 1918, with the universally hated Bolshevik régime.

Other reasons for a stronger solidity of the Magyar Dictatorship, as compared with the Italian, are, in my opinion:

— The Italian Dictatorship tries partially to cloak itself with a syndicalist ideology, borrowed from the French Sorel. More simply and sincerely, and therefore more soundly and safely, the Magyar Dictatorship rests only on feudal and national traditions. This policy is less paying from the advertising point of view, but, being more authentic, is more solid.

— Both Dictatorships are strongly nationalistic; but, whereas more emphasis is laid, in the Italian phrases, on Imperialism and on " Roman " traditions, the Hungarian Dictatorship finds itself, again, on a much more realistic plane, since the feeling that Hungary has been cruelly wronged by the Peace Treaties is universal among all Magyars. On this point, the least chauvinistic among the Hungarians, to begin with exiles like Jászi, feel not very differently from old Apponyi — even if they differ from Apponyi as to the causes and the responsibilities of the disaster. This patriotic unanimity is a force in the hands of the Budapest Government.

To conclude: While dictatorship in Italy is a house of cards which may stand, and may equally fall to pieces at any moment, there seems no reason why the Hungarian régime should end.

Sad though this may be to the many admirable Liberal-minded Hungarians who have suffered so bravely for their ideals, one is bound to admit that the present form of Government is not, historically speaking, a monstrous anachronism to present Hungary. The Spanish revolution of 1931 was mainly a movement of the cultured middle classes; nothing of the kind is conceivable in Hungary; and an agrarian revolt — a *jacquerie* — even less so.

Maybe the very violences of the present dictatorship will contribute to the awakening of a new democratic spirit among the Hungarians. On that day the heirs of the old castes will at least have learned to fight unmasked for their privileges, instead of hiding them behind the beautiful name of Hungary.

Bibliography

Bagger, E. S. — *Eminent Europeans.* — New York, Putnam, 1922.

Daniel, A. — *Das Vordringer der Agrardemokratie in Europa und die Lage des Grossgrundbesitzes in Ungarn.* — In *Archiv für Socialwissenschaft*, year 1929.

Jászi, O. — *The Dissolution of the Habsburg Monarchy.* — Chicago, University Press, 1929.

Sforza, Count C. — *Makers of Modern Europe.* — Indianapolis, Bobbs Merrill, 1930.

Szazadunk, edited by R. Vambéry. — Budapest, years 1926–1931.

VII

THE JUGOSLAV DICTATORSHIP

T<small>HE</small> Italian unity and the German unity were the
two historical fatalities of the 19th century. The same
historical law decreed that there should be again, at
the beginning of the 20th century, a Czec nation and,
for the first time, a Jugoslav nation.

The Sarajevo murder was a useless crime. Even
without it, even without the world war, the old Austrian Empire was doomed.

The Habsburg monarchy was composed, on the eve
of the war, of ten heterogeneous nationalities: German, Magyar, Czec, Slovak, Polish, Ruthenian, Rumanian, Italian, Serbo-Croatian, Slovene.

For generations the Habsburg emperors had tried
to transform all these nationalities into a solidly centralized German state; they had failed because of the
passive resistance of the non-German peoples.

Imperial Vienna achieved, however, a success
which is generally overlooked: I mean the creation of
a new artificial nationality which — a unique case in
history — did not characterize a people, but simply

a caste: if there was no Austria — Austria in herself being solely a part of Germany — there were Austrians: Austrians who, although German-speaking, had nothing German about them. They were the members of an aristocratic and official caste, chosen through centuries by the Habsburgs, among all the blue-blooded families of Europe, which had been too glad to give their youngest sons to the Empire, and get through them new fiefs and new influences. Their descendants spoke German; but neither psychologically nor intellectually were they German. They were simply Austrians — the only existing Austrians; those who remembered pre-war Europe have seen them in the imperial ante-chambers, in the Austro-Hungarian embassies, in the Austrian cavalry regiments, and, in the last years, in the Austrian navy.

They ruled Austria, and with Austria, the Italians, the Czecs, the Slovenes and the Serbo-Croats of Austria; [1] just as their Magyar cousins ruled the peoples subject to the St. Stephen's crown: Serbo-Croats, Rumanians, Slovaks.

Only one Habsburg thought to reconcile with one another, through fair treatment, all the peoples constituting with their ten different languages the Empire

[1] It is purposely that I do not include the Poles among the peoples who had been subject to German hegemony in Austria; one might say that if there was a dualistic regime in Austria-Hungary, a secondary privileged German-Polish regime existed in Austria; where the Poles had a free hand against the Bolsheviks.

of his ancestors: it is one of the tragedies of history that this man — Francis Ferdinand — should have been killed on the eve of the War by a nationalistic youth of one of the peoples which, according to the Archduke's program, would have been raised to national dignity or at least to an honorable autonomy, on the accession to the throne of Francis Joseph's heir.

Francis Ferdinand — it was his secret — wanted to do away with the *Ausgleich* (Compromise) of 1867, through which his uncle Francis Joseph had established two privileged peoples in Austria and in Hungary.

What Francis Joseph at eighty was incapable of facing — and even of thinking — his heir was determined to accomplish: with one stroke simultaneously to break up the nationalistic supremacy of the proud Magyar and to transform the bureaucratic supremacy of the " Austrian " officials into a union of national democracies in which Germans, Hungarians, Slavs, Rumanians would have become equal partners.

Vain play to reshape history with *ifs*. But one cannot help wondering what Europe would be, if Francis Ferdinand's plan had become a reality: no European war; feudal aristocratic Austria transformed into a sort of gigantic federal Switzerland; an example for some future United States of Europe or, at least, for a *Mittel Europa* with no German hegemony. . . .

Indeed, a remote but essential part of Francis

Ferdinand's plan inevitably eliminated all idea of war, and, with war, the hatreds — and the menaces of new wars — that war inevitably engenders. For, not only was he planning the unification of the Jugoslavs of the Monarchy, changing its character from dualistic to trialistic, but he also considered that perhaps, some day, even small Balkanic Serbia might become a more or less loose partner of his new Austria, no longer a German-Magyar monarchy, but a wider union of free national entities linked together by a common allegiance to the supreme Habsburg lord. After all — he must have thought sometimes — Serbia had once been a quasi-vassal of Austria's, during the reign of Milan Obrenovich, and at a time when Austria was lacking the power of attraction he was dreaming of for her.

Certainly, the love of independence is, with the Serbians, blood of their blood. But the Archduke was entitled to hope that even the Serbians of Serbia proper might have ended by envying the freedom and well-being of their brothers beyond the borders, granted of course that these did feel free and happy.

That the Archduke's thoughts did go as far as that I have from a typically Serbian witness, old Pachich. In Corfu where we shared, during the War, so many hopes and fears — beside the occasional diversion of Austrian bombardments — the Serbian leader told me more than once, when in some of his reminiscent

93

moods, that he had never trembled for the future of his beloved little Serbia as he did when he finally caught the secret thought of Francis Ferdinand.

And yet Pachich had a sort of superhuman faith in the strength, the toughness, the vitality of his Serbian people — by which he meant only his little peasant independent Serbia that had never fallen under Austrian or Hungarian masters. The wider form of Jugoslav patriotism he never understood: it was to him a Croat invention — to repeat the very words he often used with me during the war. Jugoslavism was to him first — during the war — a strategical and later on — during the Versailles negotiations — a diplomatic necessity; but I am sure that he always looked with mistrust on the transformation of what he would have had, a " Greater Serbia," into the Kingdom of the Serbs, Croats and Slovenes.

On the other side of the trenches, the hatred and suspicion Francis Ferdinand had inspired in the Magyar leaders during the last years of his life constitutes another proof that they had guessed his plans. The Magyars knew that they were the principal obstacle to the realization of the suppler and pacified Austria he was dreaming of.

One might say with only an appearance of paradox that the ideas of the murdered Archduke were only shared in Austria by the leaders of the oppressed nationalities; the very men who, when the war broke

out, succeeded in escaping from the Dual Monarchy. All of them had begun thinking of complete
independence for their nations, only when the folly
of the Austro-German autocracies created this new
fact — the war. Without the war all of them would
have felt more or less satisfied with the new federal
Habsburg monarchy Francis Ferdinand had been
dreaming of.

Early in August 1914 some influential Jugoslavs,
among them Trumbich, a noted Spalato lawyer,
were already at work in Rome. Their program was or
seemed the same which was proclaimed in the Skupshtina by the Serbian Government in November 1914:
"the unity of all our brothers who are not yet free,
Serbians, Croats and Slovenes."

Succeeding in escaping from Prague, the Czec
leader Masaryck arrived in Rome in December 1914;
Masaryck's influence on the South Slavs [2] was probably
greater than that of any Jugoslav public man. As one
of the most important members of the Slav opposition
in Austria he had stood by his South Slav brothers
at the time of the Friedjung trial, a lurid attempt
made by the Austrian Government a few years before
the war to destroy the national movement in Croatia.
Masaryck had not shrunk from bringing before the
judges the proof that the Austrian Government was
producing documents, at the trial, which had been

[2] *Jugo* means *South;* *Jugoslav* means *South-Slav.*

forged at the Austro-Hungarian Legation in Belgrade. Therefore when, in Rome, an exile like Trumbich, he said that the heroic struggle of Serbia had created a little program for all the Southern Slavs, his word and his influence were decisive. All doubts, all reservations, melted into a common official action. In reality the differences of temperament were, almost unconsciously, more important than the intellectual and political decisions. Serbians and Croats went on, seemingly hand in hand, in reality speaking two different languages.

The military defeats of the Allies on the British, French and Italian fronts brought more union in 1917 and 1918 than the early hopes of victory. In April 1918 a Congress of the Oppressed Nationalities was held in Rome.

The Resolutions adopted by the Congress proclaimed:

that each of the oppressed Nationalities had the right to constitute its own state unity (like Poland) or to complete it (like Rumania and Jugoslavia);

that the Austro-Hungarian monarchy was the fundamental obstacle to the realization of the rights of the oppressed Nationalities;

that it was imperative to wage a common struggle against the common oppressors.

Important as the Resolutions were, the fact was even more important that the Congress meant that at last the Allies had realized the dissolution of Austria-Hungary was one of the logical and essential aims of the struggle against the Central Empires.

That it had been possible to hold the Congress in Rome meant that the misunderstandings between Italians and Jugoslavs concerning their future frontiers had been cleared; or, at least, that on both sides it had been admitted that they should be. A courageous and patriotic work was done in that sense, on the Italian side, by men like Senator Ruffini, who was acclaimed President of the Congress, by Professor Salvemini, by Senator Albertini, by U. Zanotti-Bianco and by Amendola, the young Conservative leader who lost his life seven years later in a Fascist ambush. Mussolini himself, at the time a noisy but not very important newspaper editor, took some part in the work of the Congress and he strongly approved of it (no matter if with the same earnestness with which he vituperated the same work a few years later, simply because the fashion had changed).

In reality, beneath the unanimity forced on all the Jugoslav elements by the Austrian danger, it was easy for me to detect[3] — more alive than the Slavs themselves realized — the same moral divergences

[3] Italian Plenipotentiary to the Serbian Government, wandering in 1918 between Corfu and Macedonia, I had been among those who had prepared the Congress: Baron Sonnino, Foreign Minister, unconvinced, but allowing me to act as my conscience dictated.

which I had watched two years before, in Corfu, among the Croats and the Serbians.

Trumbich had come to Corfu to agree with Pachich about a common Declaration which would have shown the world that the Serbians and the Croats — and, with the Croats, the Slovenes — had decided to become a single sovereign State. Their parleys produced a document — the Pact of Corfu.

The Pact had its importance during the dark years of the war. But how different its birth had been from other historic documents marking the union of a nation. . . .

During the long weeks of the secret Corfu discussions Trumbich appeared as an Austrian to the Serbians, simply because he was struggling against Austria — with all his forces — but with an Austrian mentality and Austrian methods; for example, with his fastidious distinctions about flags, coat-of-arms, everything, in a word, which might ensure Croat autonomy. Autonomy had been for decades the only method with which to keep Croatia alive against the danger of Magyarisation; and Trumbich, in Corfu, half consciously half unconsciously, was using against the Serbians the weapons he had so well learned how to use against Vienna and Budapest.

The Serbians, who were naïvely thinking of the union as of an annexation to Serbia, watched, bewildered; Trumbich and his thesis, and his mistrust of

Belgrade were such a surprise to them. Often they complained to me. Knowing that I had expressed my pity — more than my indignation — for certain childish slogans of the Croat Committee claiming even old Italian lands for the future Jugoslav State, they told me more than once: " Do not be afraid of our agreements; after the victory it will be easy for us to bring those busybody Croats to reason. . . ."

It was difficult for me to make them understand that they were as wrong as their " brothers "; and, above all, impossible for me to admit with them that Baron Sonnino's blind foreign policy provided the Croats with some excuses. By his Treaty of London, signed on the eve of Italy's entry into the war, Sonnino had obtained from the other Entente Powers a great part of Dalmatia: his secret treaty obliged him to feel towards Serbia almost as towards a potential enemy, since Serbia was thinking of a new Jugoslav State which would necessarily have claimed Dalmatia as one of its provinces.

It cannot be denied that immediate appearances seemed to be in favor of Sonnino's conception. History had worked to emphasize the differences between the Jugoslavs. While all the nations, in Europe, are Western or Eastern, the Jugoslav nation seems divided into two parts by the ideal diagonal line dividing East and West in Europe.

Lubljana, the main city of the Slovenes, near the

Italian frontier, is one of the most Catholic centers in Europe, while Belgrade is Orthodox; Zagreb, the capital of Croatia, is a town of strong Western vitality, while Sarajevo is more Turkish than modernized Stambul. In Slovenia, around Lubljana, we find one of the most perfect developments of modern proletariat, while Serbian Montenegro brings us back to the clan system as in pre-French Morocco.

As a rule all the Jugoslavs, who until 1918 belonged to the Austrian Monarchy, had become Western Europeans, or at least they looked so. The Serbians of the Obrenovich and Karageorgevich Kingdom are still patriarchal, with the fatal result that, though the peasants who are the great majority of the Serbians, constitute one of the healthiest, most honest and most deserving collectivities I know of, the politicians, the State officials and the future politicians and the future State officials, generally returned from some hasty university studies abroad, understand and appreciate only party struggles; they have lost all the qualities of their peasant fathers and have acquired very few of the moral forces of a *bourgeoisie*. (A couple of dozens of admirable elements among them serve only to emphasize the shortcomings of the cast.)

It is natural enough that, the two parts of the nation being so different, the Croats should more and more say of the Serbians: "They are Balkanics, they are

Orientals "; while the Serbian, proud of the war record, looks with contempt on the Croat and calls him: " Austrian! "

Different they were, and are, also in the political conception of the State. Not only had Serbia been, first as an independent Principality and later on as a Kingdom, a highly centralized State; but to understand the recent errors of the Serbian Dictatorship one must keep in mind that the acquisitions Serbia had made in the East, in 1878 and in 1912, had also given her the impression that any territories inhabited by Slavs were ready to acquiesce in the Belgrade hegemony.

The national Council of the Slavs of the Habsburg Monarchy had adopted on November 24, 1918, the following proud resolution:

" The National Council of Slovenes, Croats and Serbs, in accordance with its former opinions and in accordance with the announcement of the Government of the Kingdom of Serbia, proclaims the union of the sovereign State of the Slovenes, Croats and Serbs, organized on the complete integral Jugoslav territory of the former Austro-Hungarian Monarchy, with the Kingdoms of Serbia and Montenegro into one single country of Slovenes, Croats and Serbs."

True that the proclamation which Alexander, then Prince Regent, issued on December 1, 1918, was considered by the Croats as a simple acceptance of their resolution, since it ran as follows:

101

" Your coming in the name of the National Council, that worthy representative of our broad national thought, and your announcement of its thought, and your announcement of its historic decision of November 24, by which the unification of our whole nation, and of our whole, dear, tormented fatherland is declared, fills me with deep joy. Accepting that declaration, I proclaim in the name of His Majesty King Peter I the union of the Kingdom of Serbia with the lands of the independent State of Slovenes, Croats and Serbs into a single Kingdom of the Serbs, Croats and Slovenes."

But while the Croats read " union," the Serbs understood annexation. Under the cloak of the " Kingdom of the Serbs, Croats and Slovenes " and, later on, of Jugoslavia, too many Serbians had remained faithful to the old Pan-Serbian idea.

Among the old Serb politicians, only one, Protich, seemed to understand what was necessary for a sound union. Being the first Prime Minister of the new enlarged Kingdom he tried to create an administration based on wide, self-governing autonomies.

But the Pan-Serb ideas of old Pachich ended by prevailing: and the new State was divided into provinces having no more self-governing power than a French *département*.

When Pachich, on July 28, 1921, submitted his project to the Constituent Assembly, 161 out of 419 members did not even vote — extreme form of protest. Most of them were Croats. Of the 258 who voted, 35 were against; and of the 223 who voted in favor, only ten were Croats.

The crystallized minds of the old Serb politicians did not see the danger. With his Oriental fatalism old Pachich proved unable to change the ideals of all his life. Probably Alexander did, if only because young, and because brought up abroad.

The ten years of common life between Serbians and Croats, from 1919 until King Alexander proclaimed himself a dictator, are but a long and dreary story of misunderstandings and complaints.

Figures, all the figures, spoke for the Croats: while in Serbia (and in Montenegro which is essentially Serbian) taxation amounted only to 91 dinars per head, in Croatia it was 164 dinars and 279 in Slovenia; for the public works the proportions were the same, inverted.

In the psychological field the wrong and the right were probably to be divided: both parts paid the penalty for the excess of centralization that the old Serb leaders imposed on the new State.

Perhaps the main reason why the union has proved so stormy, lies in the fact that one of the necessary members of the true Jugoslav unity of tomorrow was lacking and is still lacking — I mean Bulgaria.

Had Bulgaria formed an integral part of Jugoslavia — as she surely will some day — the internal and international difficulties of the new Jugoslav State would not have developed into such dangerous evils. Macedonia might have become a link between the two Jugoslav groups, the Serbian and the Bulgarian, while now she is a dividing field of hatreds and jealousies. Croatia would have been less suspicious of Serbia. The Adriatic question with Italy would have been less bitter.

One man, better than any Croat or any Serb, had felt and foreseen all that: Stambulisky, the leader of the Peasant party in Bulgaria, the man who forced King Ferdinand to abdication: Stambulisky, the prophetic spirit who was the first to proclaim the necessity of a Jugoslav union, and who paid for it with his life.

When, at the time of the annexation of Bosnia and Herzegovina, Ferdinand of Coburg, in agreement with Austrian diplomacy, raised Bulgaria to the rank of independent Kingdom, Stambulisky alone damped the complacent enthusiasm of the official classes for this outward success.

" The independence proclaimed in this manner," he declared in Parliament, " represents a danger for the country. It is the beginning of a policy that will inevitably bring us to war. This leaning toward Austria, contrary to the permanent feelings of the country, we shall pay for with a catastrophe."

When, with Austria's war against Serbia, his prophecy was about to be fulfilled, Stambulisky was already leader of a fairly numerous group of peasants in Parliament; for the peasant masses had answered his call, tired as they were of paying the damage for the struggles between the partisans of Austria and those of Russia. Stambulisky's war cry — the cause of the peasants' independence can only be defended by the peasants — had echoed widely. On the day the Austrians invaded Serbia, he rose in Parliament, surrounded by his group, and cried out:

" I wish victory to our Serbian brothers! "

The majority, subservient to a king who had never ceased feeling in German, covered him with insults:

" Go, you traitor, you are nothing but a Serbian! "

And he, calmly:

" I am neither a Serbian nor a Bulgarian; I am a Southern Slav."

The blasphemy — which will prove the truth of the future — had never yet been spoken in the Bulgarian Parliament.

A few months before his death Stambulisky, being at the time Bulgarian Prime Minister, wanted my confidential opinion on what was still his supreme ideal — a federal union between the two Southern Slav nations, Bulgaria and the new Kingdom of the Serbians, Croats and Slovenes. He knew that, when

105

I had been at the head of the Italian foreign policy, not only had I not been afraid of such an hypothesis but that I had considered it as consistent with the interests of Italy and of peace.

I met Stambulisky in Milan and I accompanied him as far as the Swiss frontier. To my surprise I discovered that he knew Mazzini's admirable pages where sixty years before the world war the prophet of the Italian *Risorgimento* had foreseen the Jugoslav union and affirmed Italy's sympathy for the younger Slav people.

" What Mazzini wrote is still my policy," I told him. " I consider some sort of Jugoslav unity as one of the many cases in which Italian interests are absolutely identical with wider European interests. In a full Jugoslav federation the old rancors of Austrian origin about the boundaries with Italy, about the Adriatic, and so on, will disappear; the Bulgarian element will bring more fresh air, wider horizons. Moreover, all of you, you'll become richer; and a productive Italy prefers rich neighbors."

Stambulisky knew enough of my ideas, not to be surprised. He simply said:

" But are you not the only responsible Italian who dares to declare that the Jugoslav unity is the reality of tomorrow and that Italy must not be mistrustful? "

And I:

" Perhaps; but how many Jugoslavs, be they

106

Croats, Serbians or Bulgarians, dare express your faith in a wider Jugoslav union? "

Stambulisky nodded approvingly. I did not see him any more. A few months later, on June 8th, 1923, Macedonian partisans and demobilized Bulgarian officers had him killed; he was guilty, in their eyes, of the crime of struggling against the traditional hatred between Belgrade and Sofia.

All the same, his idea remains. And his idea alone will have the force to bring real union among the Jugoslavs.

These things needed to be premised, fully to understand and appreciate the origin of this most peculiar among present European dictatorships — the personal dictatorship of a King.

We have seen that the statesmen who controlled the destinies of the Serbians, Croats and Slovenes during the first decade of their united life, were no Cavours. The situation needed men looking ahead to the future, while the Serbian and Croat leaders remained, not only politicians, but — what is even worse for a new State — provincials.

At the end of 1918, the Jugoslav State had begun

its life amid the enthusiasm of its three peoples, the Serbians, the Croats and the Slovenes. They all, from Alexander Karageorgevich, to the humblest peasant, proclaimed democracy the one guarantee of a great and peaceful future.

The main reason for the growing dissatisfaction resided — we have seen — in an exclusive centralization of power, utterly distasteful to the Croats to whom autonomy had been for generations the most cherished weapon in the struggle for liberty against Hungary.

There is no doubt for anyone who knows King Alexander — as I have known him during the most tragic periods of the world war — that when, on January 5, 1929, he entered upon the dangerous path of personal dictatorship, his motives were only motives of a perfect honesty and integrity.

First of all it must be admitted that the discussions at the Skupshtina had become every year more violent and that any possibility of a decent parliamentary discussion among the parties seemed to have disappeared for ever. Enough to recall the incident which started the deadlock, solved six months later by the King's *coup.*

On June 20, while the Croat deputies were using in the Skupshtina their customary methods of obstruction, learned by them in the Vienna *Reichstag,* an outburst of vituperation began — more violent than usual — between Croats and Radicals (Serbians).

One of the Serbians, Punisha Rachich, a violent man from Montenegro, suddenly jumped up and declared that he would no longer stand " the insults of the opposition."

And, after a moment of silence, pointing at Radich, the leader of the Croats:

" If no one has the courage to punish Radich, I'll have it." Drawing a revolver — no Montenegrin goes unarmed — he shot at Radich in front of him.

Two men were killed, Paul Radich, a nephew of the Croat leader, and another Croat deputy; and three were badly wounded, including Stephen Radich himself who died two months later in Zagreb.

In the confusion that followed, the Montenegrin escaped; but a few hours later he went to the Ministry of the Interior and asked to see the Minister. To his great surprise he was arrested and put on trial.[4]

The Croat deputies left Belgrade at once, declaring that they would never again set foot in the existing Skupshtina, and announcing their decision to get rid of the 1921 Constitution which had merely proved an instrument of Serbian hegemony.

But, even then, their dislike of all things Serbian did not include the King, Serbian as he is. In the King they went on respecting the man and — a much more important fact — the living symbol of the union of the Jugoslavs, still dear to their hearts, on condition

[4] Later on, he was sentenced, not too heavily.

their Croat autonomies were safeguarded. It was during these feverish months that one of the principal leaders in Zagreb told an American writer who is an authority on Balkan affairs: " The State is no longer a State, but two States; the only button between them is the King." [5]

Radich himself, the idol of the Croats, the man whose death had brought about the crisis, had said after an interview with the King on February 19, 1928: " Our national army, which is our national shrine, can perhaps alone furnish a generally recognized leader strong enough to expel corruption and lawlessness without mercy, destroy partisanship in administration, and overcome the political terrorism which is turning our whole country into a great penitentiary."

But the King was still, at the beginning of 1928, averse to mixing the army in politics. Radich himself reported that Alexander had answered as follows to his suggestions: " I see that the question of forming a concentration ministry revolves about personalities, and I admit that a concentration of all political parties perhaps offers the only way of solving the great questions of the hour. I shall continue to investigate this matter. On principle, I am prepared to look for an individual capable of the particular task of carrying through the proposed program of concen-

[5] *Foreign Affairs*, Vol. VII, p. 600.

tration. After that, the parliamentary parties should find a new leader in the National Assembly and should continue to work under parliamentary leadership. But under no circumstances do I want any feature of party politics to be transferred to the army."

When the Koroschez Cabinet, the twenty-third since 1919, which had been created after the Skupshtina murders, went in December 1928 to a sudden crisis due to the customary disagreements among the leaders of its majority, the King had finally grown accustomed in his mind to the idea that his duty lay in assuming direct responsibilities, with the army as his main instrument; was he not the only one to whom the Croats looked with affection and trust?

He made up his mind; he did so — I am firmly convinced of this, and my conviction springs from my knowledge of the best sides of the man — as one does to accomplish a painful duty, but a duty nevertheless. Two thoughts must have urged him on, the one and the other fallacies frequent in kings: the illusion that loyalty towards him was a feeling immutable and dynamic; the fear lest the proposed amendments tending to change the Constitution along federative lines, which were submitted to him at the time of the fall of the Koroschez Cabinet, might mean the beginning of the end of the young Jugoslav State. (With all kings, even with those whose royal rank dates but two generations back, centralizing and unitarian in-

111

stincts *à la Louis XIV* soon seem to become blood of their blood.)

Probably, a third impulse — at least as fallacious — prompted the King. Dictatorships were in existence all around Jugoslavia: in Italy, in Hungary, in Albania and even — although in a prudent and veiled form — in Bulgaria. No doubt that the Serbian generals must have been convinced in their incurable militaristic naïveté that Italy was stronger under a dictatorship than under the democratic régime which had brought her to victory after four years of the most terrible of wars; and that to start a dictatorship in Jugoslavia meant making her stronger against her dangerous big neighbor. How could one pretend that a young Balkan king should have seen more clearly, in this issue, than did his generals? It would be to expect in him the soul of a Marcus Aurelius. . . .

The Croat leaders were they who gave the King the final impression that he could no longer evade "duty" when, in December 1928, they asked him not only that the Kingdom should be divided " on historic lines," which meant the end of any form of Serbian hegemony, but that each of the new autonomous states should have not only its independent civil administration but its army as well, an army not liable for service outside the frontier of each state, except by deliberation of the local Diet.

These ideas were submitted to the King on January 4, 1929, by Dr. Matchek, the Croat leader who had succeeded Radich.

It was asking too much.

On the following day the dictatorship was decided. And on the morning of Sunday, January 6, the Serbs, Croats and Slovenes read, posted on the walls of all the official buildings, from Lubljana to Sarajevo, that the King had dissolved Parliament and rescinded the Constitution.

" The hour has come " — so ran the royal proclamation — " when between my beloved people, all the Serbians, Croats and Slovenes, and the King, there must no longer be any intermediary."

After this literary phrase, which has become an obligatory feature of any *coup d'état* proclamation, the document went on with less empty words, which, — I do believe, although events are beginning to give them the lie — represented at the time the honest intention of King Alexander.

" Parliamentary institutions which, as a political instrument, were a tradition of my regretted father, have remained my ideal as well. But blind political passions. . . ."

Unnecessary to reproduce the long page charging Parliament with all the sins of Israel; such passages are always the same; all dictatorships use almost the same words; none of them trying to explain how it is that Parliaments work admirably when faced by

113

men like a Cavour yesterday or an Asquith and a Poincaré today.

More important for the political thought of the new king-dictator was the passage concerning the unity of the State: " It is my duty to safeguard the unity of the State at all cost. I have resolved to fulfill this duty unhesitatingly to the very end. The supreme ideal of my reign is to maintain the union of the People. This ideal ought to be the supreme law not merely for me but for each individual."

When the Jugoslav dictatorship was proclaimed, many wondered, among the Westerners who know, or think they know, about the Balkans, whether the *coup* had originated with the King or with the military Serbian leaders around him.

Contrary to what has been said and believed abroad, the King is not the prisoner of his generals. His generals only share his responsibility in so far that he sounded them, as well as half a dozen politicians, on the eve of his *coup;* and all agreed with him, and especially the generals.

Alexander was not trying to show more authority than he had when he said to a Frenchman immediately after the proclamation of the dictatorship: " Whether I succeed or fail in my task, it is my own person which is at stake." And — a proof even more convincing — speaking with the same American writer I have quoted above, Alexander said a few months before the *coup,*

114

that he might unwillingly be obliged to resort to a dictatorship; " but — he added — if I do, it will be mine."

One may hardly imagine that King Alexander personally liked the idea of securing dictatorial power. Unconstitutional government cost three of his predecessors their thrones and to one of them, another Alexander — the last of the Obrenovich — his life.

Alexander Karageorgevich cannot have forgotten all that.

Moreover if he has personal energy, ambition and military spirit, he has also real democratic blood in his veins. True Serbian, he has not been accustomed to flattery, he has not been brought up in the silly atmosphere of an old Court; he has not forgotten that he is the great-grandson of an illiterate peasant, Kara Georg — George the Black — who became famous through his guerrilla against the Turks; he has forgotten even less his father, the good and evanescent Peter who, as an exile in Geneva, wrote in his preface to his own translation of Stuart Mill's *Liberty:* " The nation which is incapable of winning its parliamentary freedom is unworthy to exist." What I have seen myself of Peter, during the gloomiest days of the war, in Macedonia and in Greece, what I heard of him from one of his brothers-in-law, makes me sure of his deep intellectual honesty.

True that, for Alexander, one might point to his

education at the court of St. Petersburg, to his being the grandson of a man of strong autocratic habits, like Nicholas of Montenegro; but all this means very little to all those who, not dazzled by empty monarchical words, know the deep democratic feelings of the Serbians, and how little the Serbians — all of them — have accustomed their kings to words of flattery.

Anyone who has learned to know Alexander during the war has always felt in him the Serbian, the Serbian officer perhaps; never for a moment has either he or his elder brother George recalled to a Western mind that they were princes in a Western fashion, with the naïve illusions of Western princes; they had their Serbian feet solidly placed on reality.

No, whatever the end and the consequences of the dictatorship started in January 1929, one must admit that it was originated, in Alexander's mind, by honest intentions; and that even his illusions were not the vicious expression of a despotic spirit, but the unavoidable consequences of the situation.

His main illusion seems to have been one of an essentially military character: that to solve the quarrel between Serbians and Croats the best way was to extinguish both, merging them into a new nationality of his creation. Being himself a Serbian, he probably thought that he was giving to all an example of abnegation.

He did not realize what probably would not have

116

escaped his skeptical father: that national feelings based on long centuries of history are not to be disposed of with dictatorial decrees; and that his remedy was bound to provoke stubborn antagonisms.

True that his dictatorship was not unpopular at the start; but, after all, almost any kind of dictatorship begins with a certain amount of mass expectation. Only, the expectation in Jugoslavia was bound to make more evident the King's double failure: because the Croats hailed with delight the abolition of the Constitution of 1921, hoping that they would get an autonomous rule for Croatia; while the Serbians hoped that their King would at once appoint a juridical commission to draft a new and wider constitution.

Neither of the two expectations was fulfilled.

The good practical results of the dictatorial régime do not count sufficiently with the majority of the people to make up for the offense made against their traditions and their hopes.

After a period of marking time, the Jugoslav dictatorship introduced two reforms, which probably reflected the views King Alexander had been cherishing most with regard to the " unity " of the State.

By a law promulgated on October 3, 1929, the old designation of " Kingdom of the Serbs, Croats and Slovenes " was officially replaced by that of " Kingdom of Jugoslavia." With the childish habit of all dictatorships the use of the separate names of Serb,

117

Croat and Slovene, or of their separate national emblems, was strictly forbidden.

By another reform the State was divided into nine *banovinas* (provinces), each governed by a *ban* (governor) to be appointed by the King. This was meant to be a clever reform. It abolished about forty *oblasts* (provinces) into which the new Kingdom had been divided; and by doing so it hoped to please the autonomists; but at the same time, it was making a clean sweep of all the old historic names and divisions: Croatia, Dalmatia, Slovenia, Montenegro, Bosnia, Herzegovina. To please the Croats, even the old glorious free name of Serbia was sacrificed.

The nine banats were given entirely new names, taken mostly from rivers, according to the precedent of the French revolution, still a good pattern for purely external reforms in Eastern Europe.

The fact that the Belgrade rulers hoped for a moment that such a " reform " might constitute a new departure for national feelings is enough to prove how easily dictatorial régimes lose any psychological understanding. Indeed, to the discontent and disappointment of the Croats — and, this time, of the Serbians themselves — the Dictatorship added the feeling that an attempt had been made to cheat more or less everybody.

Another element of irony in the reform was given by the constitution of provincial senates (*banske vetche*); meant to represent organs of public will, their members are in reality nominated by the Minister of the Interior; and their power is insignificant.

Strange to say, the more immediate danger of opposition, of open revolt, is now in Serbia, not in Croatia.

The Serbians are accustomed to freedom. The Serbian officers, on the other hand, have a tradition of *pronunciamiento.* When I heard in 1930 and '31 that army commanders like Smilianich and Terzich, whose bravery and services I had been able to appreciate during the war, had retired on half pay, and with them quite a lot of other important generals and officers, I felt at once that the move had been decided upon in order to check a rising discontent in the army. But each of these measures creates centers of bitterness and vengeance, all the more important when these centers are set at work in a general atmosphere of dissatisfaction.

What was admirable about the old peasant Serbian nation was the simple and proud feeling all the Serbians had — I found it among the humblest farmers — that, through their deputies, they were the masters of the national destinies. Now, the Serbian peasant — which means nine-tenths of the nation — misses not only his old position, or illusion, of being the master; but he misses also, in practical everyday life, the contact which he used to have with the gov-

119

ernment — for his affairs and those of his village — through his elected representatives.

On the opposite side of the Jugoslav problem, the Croat peasant was not used to thinking that the government depended on him. But, if less proudly than his Serbian cousins, he liked his autonomies; in more recent years, thanks to Radich's enthusiastic propaganda, the *Seljetchka Stranka* (Peasants' Party) had become to him a link of common social life with his fellow peasants.

All these manifestations of free life have now been destroyed, in Serbia as well as in Croatia, by the dictatorship.

I have not been in Croatia since the war. But I have seen Serbia. And those who, like myself, remember free, easy-going old Serbia of the past, are struck with wonder at the depth of moral degradation and personal cowardice which has been forced upon a country so independent, by a few years of police and military terror. Friends do not trust one another any more; all political conversations are carefully avoided; no one is sure that his neighbor is not a spy or an *agent provocateur*. To loathe and despise Russian Communism is far from insuring against a charge of being a Communist. On the contrary: the general danger has one name; to be " suspected of Communism." No doubt that, just a little everywhere, there is a Communistic movement in Jugoslavia, com-

posed partly of idiots and criminals, partly of ideal-
ists, partly of fellows in the pay of Moscow. To this
Communist party, which otherwise would be politically inexistent, the Belgrade dictatorship is blindly
giving every year students and workmen, who, in a
free Serbia, would never have thought of becoming
Communists.

But the dictatorship gladly faces this danger for
two reasons: first, like all dictatorships, it is only
thinking of the present — of its present life — and
not of the future — the future of the nation; secondly,
because as long as it can pretend that it is " fighting
Communism " it is almost sure to appear respectable
and to be welcome in financial and " conservative "
European and American circles.

One might add that one of the strangest penalties
of dictatorships is that to the moral lowering of the
masses corresponds the intellectual lowering of the
leaders. Those who had applauded the Jugoslav dictatorship as a temporary and useful expedient were
soon forced to admit that the same law operated in
Belgrade with Alexander as had always operated:
even a dictator full of initial good will, as King
Alexander has certainly been, becomes the first victim
of the new régime; he thought he would be able to go
back to normality soon; and he discovers that the hour
never comes which may bring back again a stable free
government. Sometimes a poor dictator is sick of his

spies, of his secret police, of his pretended infallibility; he would like to go back to the good tottering blunders of democracy — all blunders with some remedy at hand; but he cannot; he is a victim of the interests, the hatreds, the fears he has created. Such is certainly the case of King Alexander, since I do not doubt that he is still a man inspired by the desire of serving his country.

Sometimes his internal hidden trouble is probably even greater: he knows — to repeat what I said at the beginning of this chapter — that the welding of the various layers of the Jugoslav into one is as certain as the Italian unity and the German unity were in the 19th century. But he must also, now and then, ask himself with an honest pang whether his action which he decided for the sake of the " unity " of the State, is not going to put back for decades a union which will only be the slow work of an atmosphere of freedom.

Alexander Karageorgevich will remain in history as a typical case of honest good will, fooled by an innocent belief in the efficacy of force even in the moral field.

Bibliography

Armstrong, H. F. — *The New Balkans.* — New York, Harper's, 1926.

Armstrong, H. F. — The Royal Dictatorship in Jugoslavia. (In *Foreign Affairs,* year 1930).

Machray, Robert. — *The Little Entente.* — London, Allen, 1929.

Sforza, Count C. — *Makers of Modern Europe.* — Indianapolis, Bobbs Merrill, 1930.

Wendel, Hermann. — The Jugoslav Dictatorship. — (In *Dictatorship on Trial*, New York, Harcourt, 1931).

VIII

THE POLISH DICTATORSHIP

THE Polish dictatorship in Pilsudski. And Pilsudski is the most typical of all living anachronisms in Europe.

Joseph Pilsudski started as a revolutionary Socialist, and soon became — he was then a Russian subject — the leader of a terroristic organization. His Socialism was not only more Prudhonian than Marxian, but, probably, was little more than skin deep. The Socialist label meant this, to him, above all: the possibility of recruiting Polish workmen for his conspirations against the Czar's régime.

His was the ideology of 1848 hardly adapted to the economic conditions of the nineteenth century.

This Socialist leader represented, in reality, the traditions of the Polish gentry: therefore nothing of the turncoat about him. And the Polish gentry was a turbulent class of impoverished, unpractical, indebted landowners, sometimes generous but always undemocratic — with no regard for nations and classes other than theirs. Old Poland was simply this gentry. And to understand Pilsudski it is necessary to have an idea of old Poland, not of the present one: the Poland of the dead *Respublica*, where the nobles chose the Polish representatives for the Diet, only to render the Diet's work impossible by the exercise of the *Liberum Veto*, — i.e., the right of each member to prevent by his *no* the passing of any law, even if voted for by all his colleagues. The nobility, whence came the Diet, was numerous, poor, proud; numerous — once, a whole army which had just beaten the Turks, was ennobled; poor, for the administration of estates was too mean a concern for it; proud, for the shabbiest and most *déclassé* among the noblemen knew that, legally, he had the right to be elected king.

The Liberum Veto naturally led to anarchy, to governmental impotency; nineteenth-century Western Europe was to discover the theory of the omnipotence of parliamentary majorities whereas eighteenth-century Poland, more individualistic, had discovered the omnipotence of opposition, be it of one man only.

But, since a State must live, the Poles made an even more surprising discovery. It was unworthy of a Polish nobleman to give way to a parliamentary majority; but if that majority took the shape of armed action, the same nobleman who could not, without disgracing himself, give in to votes, could give in to swords drawn against him and his followers. Two parties which appealed to arms called themselves re-

125

spectively " the armed Federation "; the lucky one which succeeded in capturing the King's person became the " Great Federation," and gave the law as long as it remained the strongest.

These Poles, the Poles of the old republic, had coined this unique and ultra-Polish maxim: " The non-existence of government is the foundation of Poland."

Strong-willed as he is, Pilsudski still seems to me the living embodiment of this sentence.

The historical tradition, changed through centuries into a sort of national temperament, has become more harmful in present-day Europe, because of the retarded independence of Poland. Poland did not regain her freedom when Italy and Germany established their unitarian states; and her retarded rebirth accentuated the shortcomings of an archeologic ideology brought to life again in a world which does not understand it any more. For instance, the present Polish militarism has nothing in common with the militarism of pre-war Germany; it is, psychologically speaking, the direct descendant of the Napoleonic militarism, or, at least, of the militarism of the French revolution.

The same phenomenon of mental persistence of things of the past we witnessed, after the war, in the diplomatic field. When the Poles, in 1918 and 1919, reappeared at the Peace Conference and in all our capitals, we found that they were still the delightful and unpractical Poles of old. Their public men flooded the Cabinets of the Entente with memorials, reports, plans, historical reconstructions, juridical theses without end. According to them, half of Europe had been Polish and might become Polish again. Poles are sometimes accused of a somewhat feminine want of logic. These Poles were terribly logical and persistent, with the result that everybody got sick of their claims.

So it happened, for instance, that when Dmowski asked for the annexation of East Prussia to Poland, to avoid, as he very logically said, the paradox of the Dantzig corridor, diplomatic Europe became so irritated with these eternally increasing demands that, had matters depended on Lloyd George alone, we might have seen in the end a Fourth Partition.

Pilsudski being Poland, he is, he must be, essentially militaristic and nationalistic; but he is not so in a vulgar way. Even his worst enemies must admit — or will end by admitting, after his death — that he represents the living tradition of a gentry which was ready to sacrifice life and riches for a great idea; an idea which remains noble even if, in a new world, it takes the form of dangerous national egotism.

It must be added that Pilsudski did not aim, in the first years of the new Republic, at becoming a dictator; in fact, after the war, he deliberately withdrew himself from the political field, concentrating only on the army.

In a moment of disgust, the old turbulent belted knight reawakened in him; he kicked Poland's feeble political edifice; everything fell to pieces. And it became almost his duty to clear the ground. The men whom to their faces he called thieves and *canaille* and threatened with the whip, replied by electing him President of the Republic. He refused the post and put into it Poland's " unknown civilian," a decent man chosen well-nigh at random. But this did not free Pilsudski of the burden and the responsibility; he could not leave the irresponsible ones he had placed in power to their own fate. Of course, years of dictatorial power, general flattery around him, and all the other fatal consequences of autocracy worked on him — on him getting older and less healthy.

But the origins of his dictatorship explain how it is that Pilsudski is hated by many, being the dictator; but, all the same, not in the same irreconcilable way other European dictators are hated and loathed. There is also, for that, an essentially Polish reason. During their generations of enslavement, the Poles had got accustomed to speaking of the government as *they*, and to hating *them*. Now they speak of Pilsudski as *he*; but there is this difference — were they to hate *him* too much they would be hating *themselves*, for we have seen that Pilsudski is the most typical personification of the Polish gentry. In him, as in a mirror, the Poles see themselves. All their qualities and short-comings are reflected in the irritable, erratic ego of their present master.

As he is now, so he was when a leader of the Polish Socialist Party under the Russian rule before the War. During the 1905 revolutionary movement he led the terroristic forces of his party in a way so opposed to any possible program of a labor organization that his central committee called him up for an explana-tion; he gave none; — instead, he simply asked, and got, absolute command of the mobilized forces of the secret organization.

As he was, so he is now. Strong, and even great (to have made Poland an important power in twelve years is a stupendous achievement), he is at the same time whimsical and neuropathic, going in and out of power according to his fits. Of one thing only he is careful — that is, constantly to keep, through his knowledge of stage effects, the impressionability of the Poles under his spell; and even that is not done out of personal vanity, but as a political necessity.

Just as he has never been a revolutionary in the common sense of the word, so now he is not a dictator like the others. All the European dictators have their origin in the interests of a caste, or of a class, or at least of a group. Pilsudski's is a dictatorship which had its origin in a sentimental spell of hero-worship.

He spent his life striving for the liberation of Poland; he gave her an army when the World War offered Poland the great opportunity; he declared himself a Socialist when he thought that it was the best way to fight Czarist Russia. In reality, — I have already said — he has always been, at heart, the tradition-made man of the Polish gentry — that troublesome class of warriors, sometimes self-sacrificing and active, sometimes lazy and dreamy, but always unpractical because their dreams were — or are? — too lofty and too distant, too exclusively imbued with the traditions of old Poland.

No use, then, imputing to Pilsudski facts and wrongs that were probably fatal; Pilsudski, let us never forget that, is Poland. And with him, with his manias and errors and fits, Poland simply pays the penalty for a crime of which she has been the victim — the partitioning of the old Polish state among robber neighbors, Austria, Prussia and Russia, with the consequence that Poland not only regained her independence generations after Italy and Germany; but she regained it only after long years of war, invasions, famine, revolution, hesitations between German schemes and Entente formulae.

Truth to tell, when prosperous countries like the United States are sometimes tempted to pass sweeping judgments on all the disorders and injustices so patent today in Polish public life, they ought to remember

130

that the United States and similar countries are spared
the sense of insecurity given by open-land frontiers,
that they have a common political origin, while in
Poland the political and intellectual education is
Russian in Warsaw, German in Poznan and Austrian in Galicia. Pilsudski's heaviest error he probably breathed in Russian Poland, where he spent
all his life — when he was not a prisoner in Russian
jails.

His immediate enemy was the *Ochrana*, the secret
Czarist police which evolved, in Soviet Russia, into
the Tcheka. Surrounded by international dangers of
all sorts, Pilsudski has not dared to rely on liberty,
but has copied the very thing he formerly most
loathed. The *Ochrana*, which he fought, has become,
in Poland, the *Defensive*. It spies everywhere; it pries
into the most intimate personal matters; and, with its
system of blackmailing and terrorizing, it achieves
the same results that analogous systems achieve in
other European nations — an appalling lowering of
the moral character of the citizens.

One may ask: " But why, with all his power, does
Pilsudski insist on keeping a Parliament, and why,
for instance, did the electoral campaigns of 1930
seem so important to him? "

The only possible answer proves that Pilsudski —
for all his outbursts and furies and, during the last
two or three years, his speeches crammed with un-

printable obscenities — has remained more prudent than certain other over-rated dictators. The existence of a Parliament (a Parliament with an opposition, of course) allows him to make the *Sejm* (such is the Polish name for the Chamber) the scapegoat for all the failures people complain of in Poland.

But all his political errors, deplorable as they are, were probably fatal.

What, in my opinion, seems Pilsudski's greatest and most personal blunder is one which contains the possibility of external conflicts; I mean the essential part he played in shaping the rash new eastern frontiers of Poland. He has no special responsibilities for the corridor which divides Eastern Prussia from the rest of Germany. But the frontiers toward Russia have been his own idea. A partial application of his old romantic dreams about White and Little Russians and about a Ukrainian buffer state under Polish direction, these boundaries are cutting so deeply into the very flesh of Russia that it will be difficult for them ever to become the sacred permanent thing the frontiers of a country ought to be.

When one comes by rail from Russia into present-day Poland, as I have done more than once, one cannot help but be struck by the symbolical difference between the two frontier stations. The Polish station is a charming stone building covered with artistic tiles; the Soviet station is simply a series of old railway carriages with a pair of bare wooden rooms that might be taken down in six hours. Pride, and a sort of gloomy certainty, show more on the Soviet side.

Keen observers who have studied the situation in these newly acquired territories, have defined them as a Polish colony under Polish military and political occupation; to call them Ireland before the days of Home Rule would convey the reality better, I am afraid.

But if England did not succeed with Ireland, it is even more difficult for Poland to curb the Ukrainians. When one knows, as I think I know, the tremendous power of resistance of the Ukrainians, their economic activity, their moral force which makes them — probably alone of all the Slavs — voluntary teetotalers (their successful co-operative stores refuse to sell spirits) one feels obliged to doubt very strongly that Poland will ever be able to swallow and Polonize these 4,000,000 men.

With a little freedom and tolerance, Poland might get rid of the Jewish problem. With a little political tact and with some international good will the friction with the Germans in Upper Silesia might some day evolve into fecund co-operation. Even the corridor to Danzig may be the object of some practical compromise. But Pilsudski's annexations will always remain a heavy problem in the future of Poland.

It is the eternal penalty of all dictatorships — they

133

think that their justification lies in " glory " and conquest.

Imperial Russia, with all her tremendous force, never succeeded in the Russification of the Ukrainians; Bismarck, with all his genius, completely failed in his policy of Germanization of the Poles. Is it true that history does not teach anything to anybody? Here we have Pilsudski's Poland repeating the same vain errors.

In spite of the violent domination of the *Defensive* all the Ukrainians are secretly working for their national dream; the poor ones dream of some sort of annexation to Soviet Russia; the Ukrainians of the middle and upper classes work for some future independent Ukrainia, created at the expense of Russia as well as of Poland, and reaching to the Black Sea.

Dreams? Possibly; probably. But even the resurrection of Poland seemed a dream to the wise ones twenty years ago.

A revived Poland has been the vindication of justice, the redressal of one of the worst crimes of the eighteenth century. Pilsudski has been, in the work of Polish awakening, one of the noblest sons of the Polish nation; Poland has many great and magnificent tasks before her. It is indeed a pity to see a brilliant nation which has known what it means to be oppressed, unhesitatingly become, in her turn, the oppressor.

A great pity — a cynic might add — not so much because it is a moral fault but because it is a political error. When a state has large zones of aliens inside its boundaries only one policy can render difficult, if not impossible, the creation of phenomena of unrest and revolution. That policy is one of tolerance, of broad autonomies, and — when autonomies are not easy to grant — of equal opportunities.

When Italy reached her natural frontiers at the Alps following on her victory over Austria, and some 500,000 Slavs became Italian citizens, the Liberal government then in power in Italy gave these Slavs the greatest freedom in the matter of schools, churches, use of their language in the courts of justice, etc. When all that was withdrawn by Fascism, a fanatical Jugoslav nationalist wrote a pamphlet to prove that, for the future of the Slav cause, the violences of the new rulers were a blessing, " while the liberalism of Giolitti and the friendly phrases of Sforza were the real danger."

Strange that all dictators always mistake an excess of violence for strength. Real strength is quiet, it is never noisy; but dictators — even when they are rich with a beautiful past like Pilsudski — always end in a childish exaggeration of police systems, of coercion even in the moral and intellectual fields.

They end by doing so even against their own selfish interests — like the drunkards who in their last

135

stages are no longer able to distinguish a good wine from a poisonous liquor.

And the drunkard, in Poland, is in a much more dangerous position than anywhere else, since he is near a precipice — Russia.

All Poland is in the shadow — for love or for hatred — of Sovietic Russia.

True that Poland seems still a long way from revolution.

But this was believed also of Russia before the 1917 earthquake.

And the revolution came to imperial Russia because, like Pilsudskian Poland, she had solved neither her national nor her economic and social problems.

As in other nations, dictatorship in Poland is strong enough instantly to crush the slightest revolutionary manifestations. But, unconsciously, it creates the germs out of which, some day, a social revolt may break out among the starving peasants, and a national uprising among the oppressed national minorities.

A true friend of Poland must advise her that it is reasonable for the Poles to be afraid of Sovietic Russia; but it might be even more useful not to forget the lesson of Czarist Russia.

Bibliography

Sforza, Count C. — *Diplomatic Europe Since the Treaty of Versailles.* — New Haven, Yale University Press, 1927.

Sforza, Count C. — *Makers of Modern Europe.* — Indianapolis, Bobbs Merrill, 1930.

IX

THE GERMAN DANGER

Nothing more difficult than to define one's impression of the present situation in Germany, the evolution of her political parties; the importance one should attribute to the two extremist tendencies which are outlining themselves there — Nationalists and Communists; — the value of traditions, to mention essential problems only.

How well one understands, and how much is it to be excused, that the Germans should be inclined to write in folios when they treat of things German. . . .

May I add that the dry and swift precision of the English language makes one understand even better the difficulties of elucidating the essential traits of a German movement? One feels tempted to own that German words alone would meet the case adequately. There always is, in the representation of a German idea, something inaccessible, because, besides the matter-of-fact part, the idea includes a search for something afar off and vague. Nietzsche tried to explain this everlasting transformation of the German soul by the multiplicity of historic elements which go to make it up; a central people indeed, the Germans are the most amazing and the most contradictory of nations; they are indefinable; which, by the way, makes their neighbors, the French, quite desperate, for Frenchmen always want to see everything clearly divided into classes and categories.

In no European country, for instance, is it so difficult to judge a public man as in Germany.

The German politician, the member of the Reichstag, is nothing but a soldier of his party. Before his election, he has gone through the ranks. He is rarely elected on his own merits as in the United States, in England or in France. Owing to the German system of Proportional Representation, the voter often does not know the name of the Deputy who, once elected, becomes a mere cell of his group. The rigidity of the parties annihilates what remains of personalities in their members. It needs an exceptional temperament for a man to survive such a soul-killing ordeal. There is only one recent example: Stresemann. And he is dead.

From a general point of view (not to be confused with the technical problems of electoral periods), only those German parties offer a psychological interest which, in the present period, are making a passionate appeal to youth. For there lies one of the most serious problems of post-war Germany; and not only because

139

the young will produce the leaders and the ideas of tomorrow. The reason is more immediate: what strikes me most in Germany, outside of political formulae which, there as everywhere, are nothing but frameworks — or, at most, distant aims — is the absence of young people in public life. Everything political is, in Germany, in the hands of old men or men of very mature age. Certainly, the disastrous results yielded by the Fascist experiment in Italy, where a generation of young men, totally devoid of experience, grabbed power as if it were booty, does not seem particularly encouraging. But Germany, after 1918, had a tremendous asset, as far as the moral maturity of her youth is concerned, in a fact which is not disastrous in all fields — I mean her defeat. Military victory is sometimes a heady beverage; defeat is sometimes a sobering lesson. If Sedan contributed so much to the creation of a democratic atmosphere in Caesarist France, especially among the young, the same thing might have happened, might yet happen, in Germany. Kept at arm's length from all real life by the mature men in power, the young take their revenge by flocking to the two extreme parties, the Nationalist-Socialist and the Communist.

Now, the Nationalist-Socialists or Nazis — their abridged name — are a sort of Ku-Klux-Klan with, however, a vague tendency against Capitalism. They pretend they want to renovate Germany by subjecting her to a hero-mysticism exalting the spiritual virtues, the worship of national energy, a new sense of human values, and destined to supplant the selfish and vulgar materialism of upper-class life. They draw their force from the dissatisfied and starving lower middle class. According to the statistics, there are at present in Germany some 30,000 unemployed University-trained students, who think that the world has been monstrously unjust to Germany (by which they mean themselves); that Wilson betrayed Germany; that the *Kriegschuldsluege*,[1] basely admitted, they believe, by a Democratic Government, is going to bleed them, and their children to come.

The leaders of the Nazi movement must have had up till the present the same second-rate but politically useful skill, first shown by the Fascists in Italy — to appeal to every form of discontent and of morbid hopes. To the peasant they have said that the peasant is the true source of German life, in contrast with the corruption of the town. To the shopkeepers of the towns they have said that their ruin comes from Big Business in Jewish hands. Officials they dazzle with the good Imperial days, when to be an official was to be a Superman. To youth they offer the mystical vision of a Germany from which all elderly men shall have been swept away, and where power and glory will be reserved exclusively to the young.

[1] The " War debt lie."

The program of the Nazi movement is worth reading; to do so, is instantly to recall the analogous program which Mussolini published in 1919, and which is now forgotten by all Fascists in Italy.

These are the main points of the Hitler program:

1. Unity of all Germans in an All-Germany in accordance with the proclaimed right of self-government of all nations.

2. Equal rights for Germany with other nations, and cancellation of the dictates of Versailles and St. Germain.

3. Germans must be of German race. Religion is of no importance in the matter. No Jew is to be allowed to be of German nationality.

4. All non-Germans who have come to live in Germany since August 2d, 1914, shall be expelled, if they live on German money.

5. Abolition of income without work.

6. Confiscation of all war profits.

7. Nationalization of all industries and firms which are already now in the hands of Trusts.

8. Enlargement and conservation of the middle classes.

9. Land reform, inclusive of possible nationalization.

10. Restoration of the conscript system.

11. German-controlled Press.

12. Strong Central Government power. Representation on the basis of ranks and interests.

Each of these points — which the leaders of the Nazis promise to " fulfill at the risk of their lives " — is capable of every kind of casuistic interpretation. The affirmation of nationalization of industries in the hands of Trusts, and of the possible nationalization of land, have already been interpreted and watered-down to such an extent that Big Business and Land-lords have continued comfortably to subsidize the Hitlerian movement, so dangerous — in words — to these interests.

This art of equivocating — to raise two conflicting hopes simultaneously — is probably the point where Hitler resembles more strikingly his predecessor Mussolini. The title of the paragraph on private property in an official Hitlerian publication:

" Privateigentum? Ja und nein! "

might be his trade-mark.

During the electoral campaign of 1930, and after, Hitler never said anything which showed he had ideas of his own, besides the usual skill of the demagogue in using catch-words. It has been impossible to elicit any answer from him as to how he thinks to realize his stupendous program of Work, Bread and Freedom for all; how he conceives his foreign policy of stopping all payments of reparation, and of rejecting the

Young plan; how is he going to regain the Polish corridor which divides Eastern Prussia from the rest of Germany? To all such questions he is ever giving one answer only: " Where there is a will there is a way."

It is not surprising that, with such a variable program, the members of the Nazi party should differ profoundly among themselves — as the Fascists did in Italy, where the Fascist Government was obliged to turn itself into a Police State, and to suppress all political discussions, not only to avoid the criticisms and indictments of its adversaries, but also to conceal the irreconcilable differences existing among the groups which had been able to bring it to power.

Nobody knows exactly what the " Dritte Reich " (Third Empire) of the Nazis ought to be. They call themselves Socialists, and, to a certain extent, they probably mean to be so: but the word " Marxist " is to them a term of opprobrium, reserved for their loathed enemies, the Social-Democrats. Their Socialism is a cheap Socialism of envy — nothing more, in reality, than anti-Semitism — that Socialism of the idiots.

Anti-Semitism is the only real link between all the Nazis. It is difficult to be united in one love, in one moral aim; it is easier to unite antagonistic groups into one common hatred.

The lesser Civil Servants who remember the Hohenzollern times as an era of prosperity, and who have

144

lost all their savings through the inflation; the retired officers who cannot forget the years when wearing the Emperor's uniform made them a superior caste; even the workmen who have been drawn to the Hitler party through their dissatisfaction with the gloomy and un-rhetorical Socialist leaders — all these groups, different as their ideas and memories are, have in common one emotional instinct: hatred of the Jews who were always, more or less, considered as " strangers," and who are now pointed at as the true causes of Germany's misfortunes. The word "*Judenrepublik*" has done more harm to the Republican idea in Germany than any other slogan or criticism.

It is through its anti-Semitism that this party, entirely financed by German Big Business, and by the highest representatives of Capitalistic interests in Germany, has succeeded in hiding its very essence under a camouflage of violent phrases and vague formulae. To put it in a nutshell, this was the slogan which appealed to many workmen whose fathers had faithfully voted for Bebel first, and after for Ebert: — Freedom for the German people from the grip of the international Jewish Capitalism, in order to establish a national Socialism for the sake of the working classes.

To turn to the tactics which have enabled anti-Semitic slogans to resound through half Germany, they have been what it was natural for them to be, in a country with the military traditions of Prussia. The party has been built up like an army, militarily trained like an army; its members boast of a soldier-like uniform, follow brass bands and Colors at demonstrations and meetings; in a word, they try to be an imitation of the old German army.

Their personal courage in street tussles is increased by the knowledge they possess that the Police forces will always be on their side, especially when they fight the Communists.

The Communists are the only party, after the Hitlerians, who increased their strength during the 1930 elections. They had 54 seats in the old Reichstag, and they now have 76; they have become the third party in Germany; all their gains have been at the expense of the Social-Democrats; as a matter of fact, the increased numbers of voters — 85 per cent went to the polls, instead of 70 per cent at the previous Election — came from the impoverished middle classes for which the Communistic program had no attractive slogans like those Hitler offered them.

Unlike the Nazis, the Communists do not represent a political danger in Germany.

What matters is, that Communism has become a factor in the intellectual formation of the young. Its doctrines shed their characteristics of hatred and violence on their way from Russia to Germany, but only to become something just as dangerous: a formula

146

still a powerful organization but nothing else, is of a wide human importance, because, were it to be proved that they have lost some of their moral force, we should be obliged to draw the conclusion that such is the penalty a party has to pay, when it comes to believe only in materialistic formulae, and discards those idealistic currents which alone are capable of making History. The Socialist party in Italy paid this penalty when, remaining deaf to the necessity for individualistic life, it went on repeating the Marxian formula like a religious community muttering its empty prayers. When, in the face of the Fascists, who had managed to hide their greed under cover of patriotic catchwords — just as Hitler is now trying to do — the strength of the Socialist party might have been useful to the moral equilibrium of the Italian nation, it was found that there was little to back it. The Socialist party, however much it could boast of morally respectable leaders, was no longer equal to its task; for, confined within lifeless theories, it went on ignoring the necessity of fighting for freedom and democracy; and that is why the cheap phraseology of ex-Comrade Mussolini was easily able to destroy what remained of its force. The defeated Italian Socialist leaders were intellectual sons of the German Socialist leaders. That is why one has the right to wonder how much of real, human force, is still behind the formidable frames of the party which, numerically speaking, is still one of the most important in Germany.

Certainly, when seeing the decadence of parties which, with all their faults, represented strong and healthy political organizations, and the contemporary triumph of the silliest and most vulgar slogans, one might be tempted to wonder whether the Germans, rich as they are in stupendous mental and moral qualities, are not lacking in any sort of political intelligence. One of the last German rulers, Prince von Bülow, admitted as much to me, when, dining together one evening in his Roman retreat, he told me of the answer he had received from the famous Holstein, the permanent Secretary of the German State Department, to whom Bülow, at the time Imperial Chancellor, had complained of the incomprehension shown by the Germans about some big diplomatic question:

"Your Highness, we are supreme in music, in philosophy, in strategy, in almost every field; is it strange if in one — politics — we are incurable asses?"

In spite of my inborn optimism, I wonder sometimes, when reading about Hitlerian successes, whether the explanation is not more tragic than Bülow and his Holstein appeared to think; whether we are not confronted with a further proof of a fatality of German history, a sort of perpetual incapacity to choose between the great roads opened to a generation. . . . Thus it happened during the Reformation: all the countries became either Catholic or Protestant; only Germany remained half Catholic and half Protestant. . . . The problem of today is where and how to discover a compromise between the feelings of the Nationalists and an International mind. And confronted with this problem, half Germany seems to take the road through Geneva, the road of International mind, hoping to reconquer the greatness of yore by a policy of moderation and patience; while the other half seems seized with the *furor teutonicus*, and thinks it easier to break, with violence, all the treaties, all the obstacles.

But, after all, one must beware of those smart intellectual formulae and of the easy play of historical analogies.

One is perhaps wiser when one remembers that, in Germany, appearances must be gauged by one standard of values, and the deeper realities (often ignored by the Germans themselves), by another.

If one takes stock of German politics since the death of Stresemann, and notes the lack of authority of the leaders, the violence of the outbursts of mistrust against the forms of democracy, one might have grave reasons for concern. But is it not unfair to pretend that the Republican, Democratic forms of the Reich were accepted enthusiastically by a majority of Germans?

Despite all appearances and manifestations to the contrary, a new spirit seems sometimes slowly to arise from the ruins of the Hohenzollern Empire.

Possibly, in France, as in the countries of the Little Entente, in England as in Italy, public opinion had adopted too lightly the cheap formula of the "Two Germanies": a democratic and pacific Germany versus a Nationalist Germany bent on *revenge*.

French and — strange to say — American visitors to Germany frequently ask: When is the Kaiser coming back? In reality, no Germans ever think of the former Kaiser; practically none ever think of the Hohenzollern. In 1931, one of the Conservative leaders went so far as to say, in a public speech: "The Monarchy is all right for the movies, but for nothing else." It is something.

Of course, from time to time, a few old Generals, a few old Potsdam officials protest that without the Monarchy there can be no true national life in Germany. But nobody takes any notice of their protests. More than that, the protesters themselves — at least certain old Court dignitaries whom I knew well before 1914 — lodge their protests out of a sort of comprehensible self-respect; but in their hearts they themselves no longer believe in a régime which fell so ignominiously, whereas they were ready to lay down their lives for it. The strength, and the weakness, of monarchies lies in that they cannot but rely on a cer-

151

tain emotional element of hereditary affection, of respect for the moral character of the Sovereign. When
this affection, this respect, disappear, the Monarchy,
even if it endures, is nothing but a rootless tree. The
first blast of wind will lay it low. In Germany, the
Monarchy no longer constitutes a political problem.

Probably the German political régime of the future
will be welded out of elements of the old and the new
Germany. That is the truth which is so difficult to
convey to foreigners, especially the French: that there
should be Germans — Stresemann, for instance, was
one — who have nothing but contempt for William II
and his old camarilla of generals and courtiers, but
who, at the same time, still revere the old Monarchist history of Prussia and the glorious memories of
the high deeds of the Imperial Army during four
years of war against a world of enemies.

Hindenburg will probably remain the noblest representative of this type of German. In truth, Germany
has been lucky with her first two Presidents: the honest and simple Ebert won to the *Reich, bourgeois*
though its régime and its framework were, the loyalty
and the collaboration of the Socialists; Hindenburg
served the Republican ideal solely through the fact
of having pledged himself to it by a loyal oath, more
efficiently than decades of Republican prosperity
might have done.

Will this Germany, " seeking to bridge yesterday

and today," to quote an image from Stresemann, be able to become quickly peace-loving and democratic, in the ideal sense of the word? I should hesitate to assert as much. But what seems evident to me, is, that even this Germany wills peace, if only because she has discovered that peace leads more surely to greatness and prosperity than the industry of war — even than victory. A pacifism denying the past is inconceivable in Germany; and Germany renouncing its army as long as Europe is bristling with armaments, that also is inconceivable; but the fact remains that all thinking Germans have realized that the ways of peace are teeming with possibilities of battles more strenuous and more fruitful — and also more intelligent — than those of Verdun.

Of course, the enormous difficulties the Germans have had to contend with (reparations, agricultural crisis, unemployment, and, most of all, inflation and financial collapse), would have been better managed by men more accustomed, in Government and in Parliament, to the vivifying struggles for freedom. But that is the penalty Germany pays for having believed so long in the infallibility of a ruler who certainly had greatness in him — Bismarck — and for having, after him, put the same naïve trust in the blind ruler, the last Kaiser.

The fault lies with this long period of long mental and political subjection, if the strong personalities —

even more necessary under a democratic régime than under an autocratic one — have disappeared from the German stage.

Even today — and this is probably one of the most serious deficiencies of a situation which otherwise may seem, on the whole, rather hopeful — the Germans entertain about the social *élite* a very different idea than the rest of free Europe.

In the free European countries, the political men, even the statesmen, are not specialists, but are, or at least should be, universal minds. How often have I not heard Balfour, for instance, deride the " Authorities.". . . For my part, if I may quote myself, I found, when I became Foreign Minister, that I frequently had to forget that I had been a career diplomat; too much knowledge of technicalities rather hindered me at the beginning.

On the contrary, in Germany, confidence, admiration, go to the specialist, to the *Fachmann*. Hence a lowering of the standard of the political staff; Stresemann was a practically unique exception; but Stresemann — I have it from himself — took good care to avoid indulging in lengthy parleys with any *Fachmann* of his Department. Bismarck's Reichstag, with men like Windthorst, saw the last of the great German personalities of the past. The materialism of the Hohenzollern period had killed them all.

As long as the *Fachmann* remains on his pedestal,

154

there is no hope of any rapid ripening of the political atmosphere of Germany. *Fachmann*-idolatry is one of the first germs of the disease from which Dictatorships come.

But many symptoms go to show, even in this troubled period of confusion and uncertainty, that the number may increase of the Germans who realize that what is wanted to save the nation is neither a Savior nor a caste of Saviors, but the general, humble will to cooperate, each according to his means, in the management of the *Res Publica.*

One of the most valuable lessons the Germans of today have learned is that given by Ludendorf, admired and feared by the whole world on both sides of the trenches during the War; and who, when peace came, gave the most glaring evidences of infantile stupidity.

It must not be forgotten that the science of a life of freedom and democracy is not learned in a day. The *Fachmann* is not born who could miraculously disprove that.

And one should not forget, either, especially when confronted with gloomy prognostics, that — after all — if the Weimar Constitution does not seem as strong as the American and British Constitutions, it happened thus in France also with the Republican Constitution of 1875. For a long time, it seemed Republican, but it was not Democratic. Only after a quarter of a century did the Catholics rally to the Republic; and even today some of them still resent that Pope Leo XIII forced them to give up their monarchical tendencies.

How should things progress more quickly in Germany than in France, where the Republic was the third of its kind to be experienced by the French people?

The study of the evolution of German public life must be spread over a fairly reasonable number of years if we wish to draw a lasting lesson from it.

The difficulties arising out of the present period teach one moral for which the free nations should be grateful; that, even for a people as intellectually, culturally and socially gifted as the Germans, nothing can take the place of the exercise of freedom.

Bibliography

Die Neue Rundschau. — Years 1930 and 1931.

Hamilton, C. — *Modern Germanies* — London, Dent, 1931.

Koch-Wever, E. — *Radical Forces in Germany.* — (In *Foreign Affairs,* year 1931).

Unruh, F. F. von. — *Nazional-Socialismus.* — Frankfurt a. M., Societäts-Verlag, 1931.

X

THE RUSSIAN DICTATORSHIP

Russia has always been unlike other European countries. Her revolution and her Soviet dictatorship are equally unlike other revolutions and dictatorships. Race, climate, geographical size, Tartar domination followed by a state of serfdom, and submission to autocracy as well as to police rule — are the main causes of this difference.

Count de Maistre, the most far-seeing of European diplomats in Napoleon's day — Envoy of the little Italian State, Sardinia, to St. Petersburg — was alone in predicting the possibility which became actual fact a hundred and five years after he had prophesied it.

"There are," he wrote in 1812 to the King of Sardinia, "so many presages of revolution in this country that I quake in every limb to think of them. Can this armed people ever go back peaceably to their original state? Will they lay down arms as easily as they laid down the spade and mattock? Will this scattered peasantry starving in the forests . . . become submissive slaves once more?"

They became so then; but, a century later, in 1917, it was far otherwise.

The Russian people are at the same time the protagonists and the victims of the Russian Revolution; and in this respect they are a striking contrast to the case of the two greatest European revolutions — French and English — where the fanatical zeal of one revolutionary group succeeded in forcing a fanatical doctrine on the masses; Puritan in England, Jacobin in France.

In Russia the Kremlin was worth studying when it was inhabited by Lenin or even by Trotzky. The group of men who now dominate Russia are able to retain power only by all kinds of police measures, by exiling their enemies or putting them into prison. Intellectually speaking, they do not awaken the least interest.

In spite of the Red atmosphere, it is the old Russian story going on still.

What else did Trotzky try, in vain, to do, a few years ago when he attacked Stalin and the other men in power, than to repeat what the Liberal bourgeoisie did to Czarism, and what, later on, Lenin did to Kerensky?

The only difference, probably, consists in this: that Stalin and his comrades, who now govern Russia, are resolved to offer, from the Kremlin, a much more serious resistance to any attack than the Czar offered to Kerensky, or, later on, Kerensky himself offered to Lenin. Dictators of this sort are not " in power "; they are intrenched in power.

If we want to look briefly at the essential factors of Russian life and Russian revolution, it is better to put on one side the government and the struggle around the government, and simply study this: the present state of mind of the workmen and the present state of mind of the peasants — and their reciprocal force and position.

What are the relations between the masses of Russian workmen and the Soviet Government?

Let us begin by stating the real numerical proportion of the workmen to the rest of the Russian people, on the one side, and to the Communist party, which actually dominates that people, on the other.

The Russian workmen constitute a maximum of 15,000,000 in a total of 130,000,000 Russians, now practically all peasants. The Communist party, which had no more than 30,000 adherents when in 1917 it came into power, actually has some 800,000 members. Indeed, it might have increased to millions, as always happens when a country has fallen to such a low level that one may be sure of some measure of personal safety only by being a member of the dominant party. However, the Communist party still has no more than 1,000,000 members; but certainly not because of lack of applicants. The reason lies in the traditional respect for an old formula of Lenin which prescribed " Quality, not quantity." Be the quality bad or good, in a Communist sense, the fact is that admissions into the party are still relatively slow.

Of the approximate 800,000 members of the Communist party today, only 350,000 are workmen or ex-workmen, the others being ex-bourgeois, assumed workmen, and, in the lowest portion, peasants.

There are books in America and Europe that describe the privations and sufferings of the Russian workmen. The description is exact, the coloring not overdone, but the books are false. Why? Because they do not say a word about the real feeling of the workmen, which is still a sort of religious, unshaken faith in Communism.

Let us state the truth as it is. The Russian workmen have a profound belief that, in spite of tragic deceptions, the Leninist formula, a " Proletariat's Dictatorship," is the key to the enchanting world they hope for.

This formula they find repeated, everywhere they go, in a hundred different forms. At evening meetings, at the new free open air theaters, at the " movies," they are constantly lulled by the same refrain: " Is it not the Russian proletariat alone that rules the destinies of a great nation? Where in the world except in Russia do the bourgeois and ex-bourgeois tremble before a real workman? Where, outside of

Russia, are Imperial Palaces turned into homes for old workmen? "

The Russian workman does not yet seem tired of such courtly flattery. And, like the old guests of the Imperial Palaces in the Crimea, now turned into rest-houses for the old proletarians, he readily listens to the pleasant lullaby. He does not deny that today he is suffering, but he tightens his belt and hopes that tomorrow everything will turn out all right.

There is — and those who are unable to see it are to be pitied — some moral nobility in their thinking and saying, as they often do, that it is for their sons that they are waiting; that it is their sons who will be happy and free in this life. It is the mystic nature of the Russian soul, which is longing for suffering, which makes this possible.[1] It is with a sort of religious ardor that the working classes of Leningrad and Moscow believe themselves to be the vanguard of a new world, of a happier humanity. When they suffer, they find some consolation in thinking that, through what they are enduring, they advance the blessed days of universal happiness — the happiness of all the slaves and pariahs in West and East.

This feeling may fade. But to have deliberately

[1] Longing for suffering and accustomed to suffer. No other European nation has the record the Russians have of long successive floods, famines, pestilences.

ignored it, not to have taken it into account at all, is simply to repeat the errors of the British and the Germans during the French Revolution. They believed they could dispose of it with a simple definition — brigands.

It is strange that such a psychological factor should have come to exist, in a country where the historical materialism of Marx is meant to be the official truth, and that this fact has been denied or not understood in the countries and among peoples where the boast of a richer spiritual life is more frequent.

For my part, when in Russia — especially the Russia of the Five Year Plan — I was constantly struck with the impression that I was watching the flowering of a new religion; a religion half revelation and half business, but still a religion. It is our forgetfulness of the fact that — no matter whether it be lasting or ephemeral — the events in Russia are essentially of a religious nature, which explains why our judgments on Russia are so often at fault. To say that Communism has taken away all gayety and freedom from life, is to forget that the same thing happened at the birth of other creeds. To say that Leninism is without justice or pity is to say what must frequently have been the case in the first stages of a new religion. To say that Communism is formulated by a violent minority of fanatics, simply means that its character is that of a sect rather than a political party, and that

Lenin has in him more of a Mahomet than a Danton or a Marat.

But, if this is essentially true of the Kremlin's occupants, and the workmen, it is quite otherwise, probably, in the case of the peasants. And not a few weaknesses and self-contradictions on the part of the Russian Government — probably, also, what most essentially decided them to launch on the big undertaking of the Five Year Plan — are solely explained by the fact that an opposing force confronted the workmen and their religious dreams; and that the Kremlin felt itself dangerously situated between the two antagonistic currents.

The element antithetic to the workman was — still is — the peasant.

The peasants were " Communist " after the Revolution; or, to be more exact, they seemed " Communist " when it was a question of driving the old proprietors out of their estates. It was a repetition of what has taken place in peasant movements in many countries, from certain ancient revolts in China to the *Jacqueries* of old Royalist France.

The phenomenon seemed more formidable in Russia only because the peasant movement identified itself — in time and methods — with the Lenin *coup*. To tell the truth — and this is a point whose meaning has no little importance in the understanding of the Russian Revolution — the Russian peasant had begun, even before the advent of Bolshevism, to seize the lands and to slay his " Barin "; frequently to slay him and, in the Russian way, to weep over him at the same time. When Lenin grasped power, he simply put into words what the peasants had already begun to put into deeds. That is why the peasants supported Lenin, but without giving any serious attention to his theories.

The same phenomenon took place when they victoriously opposed the Wrangel and Denikin expeditions; they did not so much obey orders from Moscow as their own instincts, which put them on guard against young White Russian officers, the sons of the landowners they had slain some months before.

On the morrow of the World War I was in Constantinople as High Commissioner. As soon as the Italian officers attached to the General Staff of the White army reported to me that many of the Russian officers had organized raids on neighboring properties which once had belonged to them, hoping to take them away from the sons of their old serfs, I realized at once — and said so to the Big Four in Paris — that the White Russian expeditions were doomed to failure.

But even Lenin had his big failure with the peasants.

Thinking himself all-powerful, he cried in a famous speech:

" The peasants ask to be free to sell their grain.

This freedom means also the freedom to speculate. Why do they not understand that it is impossible for us to allow that? It would be the end of our Revolution. We shall never agree; we would die rather than yield on this essential point."

The peasants said — or rather, thought — in their turn:

" The land is ours, but the grain is yours; the meadows are ours, but the harvest is yours." They drew their conclusions. The result was the terrible famine which caused the death of so many millions of Russians. Hardly half of the Russian soil had been cultivated. . . .

Lenin had sworn to die rather than to yield. He thought better of it, and he preferred to yield without dying.

Among the peasants — who are the same everywhere — one finds little religious ardor for the new ideas — that religious ardor which still exists so strongly among the workmen. I myself, in Siberia, near the Mongolian borders, heard an old Kulak (rich peasant) say:

" The Bolsheviki tell us that we may suffer now, but it is our sons who will be happy. Well, we gained more with our old Popes. They used to preach that we may suffer now, but that *we* will be happy in paradise. It was always a gain for ourselves."

The peasants constituted the force of the Revolution when, towards the end of the War, they deserted the trenches and seized the lands of the Barins. But all that — the desertion of the trenches as well as the occupation of the lands — was done for essentially peasant reasons, which had nothing to do with the Bolshevik reasons and ideologies.

The real protagonist of the Russian tragedy will always be the Peasant — and Bread.

Stalin himself, in a speech delivered at Moscow in October, 1928, declared:

" So long as Russia remains a land of small rural producers, she will be on an economic basis more favorable to Capitalism than to Communism."

It was in order to avoid, above all, the danger of the Mujik wedded to his bit of land, and the Mujik turned into a Kulak, that Stalin and his followers took up the study of agricultural industrialization, the creation — as it was picturesquely put in Moscow — of " Wheat factories," where workmen could operate so as to have every possible advantage over individual peasant holdings.

It is this struggle, even if silently conducted, which will probably decide the vitality of the Communist régime. If Bolshevik proletarians succeed in producing wheat on the Russian plain, it will, for the time being, put an end to the only danger which might some day menace the Dictatorship of the Kremlin — the free Russian peasant, i.e. ninety per cent of the Russian population. If the Mujik is destined to lose, it will be the greatest triumph of Bolshevism since the Revolution of October 1917.

The old economic order is, probably, being defended today by the Russian peasants, who are fighting for their lands, and who do not guess at, nor care about, the world-wide importance of their resistance. If they are defeated, it will mean — why disguise what seems to us the truth? — that the Russian experiment is well on the way to become an historical reality; a reality which we may fear, or approve of, but the life-force of which it would henceforward be childish to deny.

It is the solution — or, at any rate, the compromise — which is eventually found for the agrarian question, that will decide whether or no the over-lauded and over-dreaded Five Year Plan is to be a success — to outward seeming, at least — or an evident failure.

Compared with this, all the other numerous industrial aims and schemes of the Plan on which the pro-American craze of the Soviet Leaders bases such hope and such pride — they take Ford to be the greatest living American — will count as nothing.

It was the staging of the Five Year Plan that suddenly aggravated the agrarian question, obliging as it did the Soviet Government to have recourse to inflation, and to obtain fresh resources by means of mass exportation.

Inflation is easily managed by an autocratic Government.

Even for the ruthless Kremlin rulers, it was not so easy to improvise an exports policy. The goods to be exported needed to be in sufficiently large quantity, so as to insure the payments to be made abroad. Only cereal exports would meet the case; but the peasants refused to sell these to the State at the prices fixed by the State itself, as they could not get their equivalent in indispensable manufactured goods, at reasonable prices.

Driven to export at all costs, the Soviet Government found itself forced to appropriate at all costs the produce of peasant labor. Hence, the idea of the "Wheat factories." To found them without open recourse to expropriation of the peasants, Stalin took refuge in the formula of "Collectivization."

The experiment of collectivizing agriculture dates from the spring of 1929. It was intended to be a co-operative movement on a voluntary basis. The Seredniaks — middle-sized cultivators — would, it was believed, stand out from the plan. Yet, contrary to all expectations, rich and poor cultivators alike were, or seemed to be, attracted by the plan, especially in the wheat area. Whether or no the prospect of raising the level of production by means of tractors and machinery really appealed to them, or whether they were scared by the growing insecurity of their own opposition, is difficult to say. Probably both elements existed, and the second much more than the first.

The agrarian program of the Five Year Plan had envisaged collectivization for about twenty per cent of the arable land, during a period of five years. How was it possible to fix on a percentage of collectivization, and yet retain its voluntary character as though it were willingly adhered to by the peasants? Who could have foreseen that, in the course of the coming five years, some four and a half million peasants, individual petty holders, would realize the advantages of cooperation and collective work?

In fixing the percentage of collectivization at twenty per cent, in five years, the Soviets saw the matter from another angle. They never for a moment thought of the free-will of the peasants; but only of the supply of technical methods (tractors, etc.) at their disposal for distribution to the *Kolhozi* (collective farms).

As the necessity for increasing the exports became more pressing, it was decided to speed up the collectivization. Having originally ignored the factor of " peasant free-will," Stalin in turn threw overboard the " technical " factor. What if Russia lacked sufficient agricultural machines to increase the yield of cooperative agriculture? No matter. The scheme should be carried out by the simplest, most primitive

169

means, down to wooden ploughs. The plan must surpass itself. The creation of " Wheat factories " must keep place with the exigencies of export trade. The *Kolhozi* must be transformed from labor communities into actual State farms.

In October 1929, that is, in the first period of the Plan, orders were given to speed up the collectivization. But, by January 1930, this proved not to be enough. The whole of agriculture, it was declared, " could " be collectivized in a single year. And, to say that it could be done, meant that it must.

Sure enough, in about six weeks time 50 per cent of all the individual holdings belonged to the *Kolhozi*. The mentality of the Russian peasant seemed changed in a few days. " Enthusiastically " — so said the official reports — he espoused the notion of collective work. In some parts of the country, " Socialist enthusiasm " — again an official quotation — led the peasants so far that they joined the *Kolhozi* in the proportion of eighty per cent . . .

But, signs of peasant discontent began to appear; optimism immediately vanished from the reports. Stalin, like Lenin before him, frightened by the great Unknown, changed his tactics. On March 15, 1930, a decree was issued forbidding forcible methods of collectivization, denouncing those officials whose heads had been turned by success (the very officials who a few months before had been most appreciated for thir Sovietic zeal), and "authorizing" those peasants who had been enrolled in the *Kolhozi* against their wills to come out of them. The percentage of collectivized lands fell at once to ten per cent, and, in certain regions, even lower.

In the autumn of 1930, the need of foreign money to pay for foreign imports became so imperative, that Stalin was forced to export, not cereals alone, but everything on which he could lay hands, including soap — on which Russian citizens have ceased to set eyes — etc. This, however, was not enough. And once again, wholesale collectivization became the order of the day.

This had continued throughout 1931. According to Russian official publications, become optimistic once more, the percentage of the collectivization has been going up with unwavering steadiness.

For us, skeptical students of Bolshevik as well as of anti-Bolshevik statistics, it suffices not to forget that, when Stalin authorized the peasants to come out of the *Kolhozi*, the percentage of collectivized lands dropped to ten per cent.

We must, then, note that the Five Year Plan hit the peasants in two places; as consumers and tax-payers, as well as producers.

The consequences of this anti-peasant policy are easily divined. From an economic point of view — the lowering of the status of agriculture, and the decline

171

of production in which the peasants, forcibly enrolled in the *Kolhozi,* take no further interest; and, from a political point of view, the increasing antagonism between the interests of the peasants — the enormous majority of the population — and the interests of the State — consequently of the Revolution itself. The struggle of the peasants against the Stalinian policy of the Five Year Plan is probably not over. The future alone will show whether it is going to be strong enough to endanger the Dictatorship of the Kremlin men. It has seemed to me, at all events, that it was not without a symbolic meaning to relate the recent developments of this silent struggle, since I happened to know them. Less meaningless, anyhow, than going on with the usual sickening generalities and guessings about the Russian situation. A former Russian ambassador talking with me about the Five Year Plan, wondered whether the Bolsheviks were aware of the existence of the famous Quinquennium Neronis — the portion of Nero's reign in which he applied himself to bettering the inner administration of his Empire, and actually alleviated slavery; five years within which, at the same time, he murdered his mother Agrippina, and his relative and political rival Britannicus, and began his persecution of the Christians.

But the comparison smacks of literature — and of political hatred.

Better comparisons may be drawn from the very history of the Muscovites themselves, since — as I said at the beginning of this chapter — the old Russian story continues to unfold itself, even in Sovietic Russia.

Early in the eighteenth century, the Emperor Peter the Great built in the swamps of the Neva a beautiful city, which he made his capital — St. Petersburg, now Leningrad. The building of this city opened a new era for Russia. It was the starting-point of a fresh epoch in her history. But, can we forget that to make this city the Czar Peter sacrificed tens of thousands of Russian peasants, who died in the swamps under the whip of the overseers, or as a result of disease, not otherwise than must have happened to multitudes of Egyptian slaves when they built the pyramids.

Those Socialists who act as did the Czar Peter, or condone such actions, are only preparing the arguments for the most terrible indictment of Marxian Communism. Besides, St. Petersburg — bought as it was with human lives — had at any rate been erected on solid and deep-driven piles. The generations who followed reaped some benefit from the terrible sacrifice of the former ones. It is, unfortunately, probable that Stalin's St. Petersburg, erected on the shifting sands of an impoverished people, will not even be of much use to future generations; certainly, the gain will not be proportionate to the sacrifices entailed —

above all, the moral sacrifices: I think chiefly of the new, menacing form of general serfdom which cannot fail to produce a ghastly moral degradation in the whole Russian people.

No doubt, the Soviet Dictatorship has in itself something more than mere terror; but terror and violence are among its chief instruments.

The great majority of Russians had never known freedom. It is a fearful truth that, even today, they neither miss nor prize it.

Yet it would be unjust to compare a movement, fanatical, yet not without a certain Messianic grandeur, such as the Russian movement, with certain other Dictatorships; which, while suppressing all liberty as in Russia, are destitute of the faintest social or spiritual aim; they suppress liberty in order to retain power.

The worst of the Russian situation in this: while there is no doubt that the Italians — like the Spaniards yesterday — will sooner or later reconquer an atmosphere of freedom, it is difficult to see how Russia is going to evolve a system of government less contemptuous of individuality and liberty.

It seems rash to expect this evolution from the errors of the Sovietic Government. Their principal mistake will probably turn out to have been the Five Year Plan, with its mishandling of the peasants. Contrary to the antithetic opinions now shouted throughout the world, I believe neither in the success nor in the obvious, immediate failure of the Five Year Plan. Most probably what will happen is this: the Soviety and their apologists will boast that the Plan has succeeded; and technically, literally, they will be not so far wrong, perhaps. Only, Russia will emerge from it poorer, hungrier, and more degraded than before.

If I am right in my surmise, the campaign against an imaginary commercial and agricultural invasion by Russia started in 1930 and 1931 in certain European and American spheres, for fear lest the Five Year Plan should prove successful, appears foolish — foolish, just as all anti-Bolshevik campaigns conducted from abroad have, practically and morally, always been.

For my part I declared this publicly when, as head of the Italian Foreign Policy, I was approached in an effort to obtain Italian collaboration in a certain anti-Bolshevik action.

" The attacks from outside " — I said in the Italian Parliament — " will never be a solution. I believe in Democracy and in Liberty, and that is why I am against Bolshevism. But to be a useful lesson to the world, Bolshevism has to die of itself."

And if anyone cared to ask me — since I am so firmly against Bolshevism — whether I do believe that nothing beneficial can result from the Soviet

Communistic experiment, I could only say that such kinds of questions are much the same as asking whether the downfall of the Roman Empire was a success and what good it did. . . .

How can one appraise an event of such magnitude?

One might however risk adding: that among the causes which brought about the downfall of the Roman Empire not the least was the feeling of deliverance roused in the souls through the spiritual revolution caused by Christianism; and that it is difficult to see how the collective slavery — psychological and moral — which appears to menace Russia can aid the upward trend of the spirits, as the Christian revolution succeeded in doing.

All else, failing this, is dust and ashes.

Bibliography

All the books on Russia I went through struck me as being biased in one sense or the other. My main sources of information on Russia, besides my personal recollections, are the official periodic publications of the Soviet government, which I constantly study; to an Italian, accustomed to read between the lines of the Fascist publicity " Documents," they are probably more illuminating than to others.

The London *Economist* and the New York *Foreign Affairs* for the years 1930 and 1931 contain some interesting articles on the Five Year Plan and other Russian problems.

XI

THE SOVIETIC IMPERIALISM

WHEN one considers the way the Sovietic Government is at work in Asia — in Persia as in China, in the Dutch Indies as in British India and even in lonely Tibet — one cannot help thinking that Russia is at work there, as if she possessed two faces, two souls.

The more I think of it, the more, for my part, I find in this sort of double personality the only explanation of the carrying on of a complex work where the semitic revolutionary spirit, which constitutes a part of the Moscow mentality, mingles so well with the imperial traditions of the old aulic Russian diplomacy.

One of the souls at present inhabiting the Kremlin is the soul of the Third International, which now directs its intrigues from Moscow only because it found it impossible to direct them from Berlin, as it had wished and hoped to do immediately after the World War. Doubly Orientals — being Russians and, many of them, Jews — the heads of the International imagine themselves to be simply under a tent at the Kremlin, hoping still that some great movement, pro-

177

voked by their unconscious allies, the Imperialists and Fascists of Western Europe, with their antiquated aims, will make it possible for them to move towards Germany, or Italy, or may be, even England.

The other soul, the other tendency, still clings to the traditions, the mirages, the ambitions of pre-war Russian diplomacy, which, probably unconsciously, had as one of its cardinal rules, to seek success in Asia when failure threatened — as it does now — in Europe.

Strange as it is, this moral and political double conscience is not unique in history. Taking into account the fact that no historical analogy or parallel is ever quite exact, this sort of dual Russian personality reminds one of the precious gift bestowed by divine grace upon the British people: — the simultaneous action, in those islands (when a great British interest is at stake), of statesmen and diplomats coolly working to obtain some most concrete political advantage and, on the other side (and without any previous base secret understanding), clergymen and writers eloquently busy showing the highest moral reasons for supporting the diplomatic action which is going on in Downing Street. Such was the case of the Belgian Congo: Belgian rule had been in force there for years; but, at a certain moment, gold was discovered in the Katanga, the Congolese province nearest to the British South African possessions; and bishops and other pious persons started at once a violent press campaign to stigmatize the Belgian atrocities against the negroes. What is astonishing and really imperial is that those bishops and other pious persons were inspired by the most perfect Christian good faith, and that nobody was pulling wires behind them.

The treaty concluded between the Soviet Union and Persia is, for instance, a retort of the Third International to the struggle waked by Downing Street against them and, at the same time, a new move in the traditional Russian struggle against England at Teheran. This treaty has been diplomatically important for the whole of Europe, as it automatically swept away all British influence from Teheran.

It is worth while to study the Russo-Persian treaty from two points of view.

When the new Shah seized the throne he was an enigma to the accredited diplomats at Teheran. At that moment he enjoyed a strong support from the British. A few private English travelers and merchants who had given vent to their distrust concerning the phrases of sympathy uttered by the new Shah incurred the open displeasure of their Legation. The British had decided to base their influence on the old Cossack officer who had suddenly become Shah. As it was a policy based on persons, not on deep permanent interests, it was bound to fail. Nothing indeed is so uncertain in the East as to rely on persons.

The Soviet policy was far more subtle.

They solemnly renounced the rights that the Capitulations afforded them in Persia. All Soviet citizens became in Persia subject to the Persian tribunals. Persian "*amour-propre*" was deeply flattered. Moscow appeared as the great possible ally against European influence. When the Russo-Persian treaty was concluded, Moscow reaped the benefit of her skillful tactics.

Stalin's idea, to group under Moscow's guidance all Asiatic nations, scored a real advantage after the losses incurred in China where Bolshevik influence had so rapidly decreased, after a short period of success based only on appearance.

For England, where Persia had always been considered as a bulwark for India, it was a loss, not so much a material one as a symbolical and moral one.

England's moral and political losses in Eastern Asia, where she used to be pre-eminent, have been even heavier.

Apart from the actual imperialistic penetration of Russia in Manchuria and Mongolia, which deserves to be studied in some detail, — the two Russian souls, the two Russian faces, merge to work, in the whole of China, for one object, one goal. This goal is the struggle against England, hated when she is Tory, loathed when she goes Labor.

Of course, it is possible that the Russia of the Third International actually did hope to establish Communism in China; this is within the realm of possibilities, although to anyone who knows the Chinese world it would be almost sure proof of a lack of political intelligence on the part of the successors of Lenin and Trotzky. It is at any rate incontrovertible that the second Russian personality, which in spite of Bolshevism consciously or unconsciously still maintains the hatreds and traditions of the old Russia, hoped by the spread of these doctrines to deal a death blow to England, the twice-hated, the two-fold enemy; firstly, because she is the living symbol of European liberalism, the conception most hostile to Bolshevism existing on the old continent; secondly, because she is England, the mistress of India and the seas, the hidden but nevertheless real protectress of the small new Baltic states, Finland, Esthonia, Latvia.

What does seem amazing, from a psychological point of view, is that, in spite of the great zeal of the agents of the Western Powers in China in their fight against Soviet action, no use has ever been made of such definite facts — facts particularly likely to appeal to the Chinese mind which always reacts to anything visible and tangible. The anti-Bolshevist campaign of the Western Powers in China has been conducted throughout with the most complete mis-understanding of the Chinese character.

I happened to be in Peking immediately after the police raids on the Russian Embassy made by Chang Tse Lin, the once famous Manchurian Tuchun, with the secret encouragement of some foreign Legations. I was able to examine many of the seized documents. Although I have always been very doubtful as to the authenticity of the famous Red Letter which won for the Tories a British general election, I am absolutely convinced of the authenticity of the documents seized and published in Peking.

These documents had all the hall-marks of authenticity, both in word and in spirit. They consisted of a series of pitiable spyings on diplomatic codes, on visitors to the foreign envoys, and of corruption of petty officials, European and Chinese. They all bear the stifling characteristics of the old Czarist police — only a little more vulgar and silly. But all this — even the military instructions and the proof of the dispatch of ammunitions — did not and could not have the least influence on the Chinese. They looked and read; half of them smiled and the other half admired. They were but oriental tricks and lies against Westerners, all these Russian activities. Why should the Chinese have felt disgust or irritation?

Different means should have been employed in order to affect the Chinese. The effort should have been made to touch their "*amour-propre*," always so sensitive. Emphasis should have been laid on the fact that the Russian "sacrifices" so cleverly advertised every day by Soviet agents were far from what they were cracked up to be. Instead of having sacrificed pre-war rights, the Russians merely accepted their loss, incurred, like the German losses, as a result of defeat in the World War; they knew that they could never hope to recover their lost extra-territorial rights in China. But it is an astounding fact that, in spite of, one might almost say, under cover of, the campaign against "unequal treaties," Soviet Russia should be the only nation in the last five or ten years to have considerably increased its privileges and monopolies as a result of its action in Mongolia and Manchuria. While the treaty rights of all the other Powers were disappearing, Russia won to herself new spheres of influence, not unlike what might have been won prior to the Hay formula of the Open Door.

Either the disguised annexation of Mongolia, or the sovereign rights exercised over the Chinese Eastern railway, if cleverly exposed, should have been sufficient to open the eyes of the Chinese as to the extent of Russian "sacrifices" and as to the truth of Soviet "disinterestedness" in China.

Let us consider these two definite points, Mongolia and Manchuria, where the work accomplished and still being done would not be disowned by any former

Imperial Ministry of Foreign Affairs at St. Petersburg.

Nowhere may the continuity of the Czarist and Red diplomacy be better seen than in their dealing with the autonomy of Outer Mongolia. The Russo-Chinese agreement of 1915 had succeeded in establishing "the exclusive right of the autonomous Government of Outer-Mongolia to attend to all the affairs of its internal administration," but, on the other hand, had again recognized China's suzerainty.

When an occasion arose, Chicherin followed faithfully the policy laid down by his predecessor Sasonow. He created a dummy "Independent Mongolian Government" the head of which was simply a certain Bodo, formerly clerk at the Imperial Consulate General at Urga, and had him ask Moscow to send troops to Urga to "defend Mongolian autonomy against China," although China was certainly, at the time, unable to assert any of her rights. Chicherin replied that he was glad to help the new Mongolian "Government." Russian troops went at once into Outer Mongolia.

Probably they would have come on any pretense. But — it is always interesting to note such things — the example had been set by a previous act of violence on the opposite side. It was Baron Ungern at the head of a band of White Russians who had invaded Mongolia and first driven out the Chinese from Urga in

184

order to create there a military base against Bolshevik Siberia.

Now, besides all the power they have got in Urga, the Russians have surrounded Outer Mongolia with a Chinese wall much more effective than the old one which, below the plains of Inner Mongolia, ends, after so many thousands of miles, in the Yellow Sea, on the Shanhaikuan beach. That is why it is so difficult to know exactly what is going on in Outer Mongolia. The Chinese Government itself likes to surround it with silence. This is a typical example of the Chinese spirit. Nanking prefers, like old Peking, to ignore, when it can, the blows to its " *amour-propre* " which it is forced to endure.

Among the many and contradictory rumors which one hears I shall only state those facts which I have been able to verify myself through repeated contacts with Mongolians whom I met during a recent stay of mine in Manchuria.

Soviet banks, established by the Russians who have become the real masters of the country, have forced the Mongolians to hand over their ingots of silver in exchange for Russian paper money.

A small Mongolian army has been created under the command of Russian officers.

Every possible obstacle is put in the way of commercial intercourse with China; all the country's resources are being artificially directed toward Siberia.

Bolshevized Buriats from Siberia are being transformed by sleight of hand into Mongolians; and it is they who play the part of representative Mongolians when there is the slightest demand for such services.

Rich young Mongolians are removed by force from their encampments and their flocks and are transplanted to Moscow, there to be fed on Soviet pap. Some of them return to Mongolia with women picked up on the streets of Moscow and with horrible diseases. From encampment to encampment this is spoken of as living proof that the Lamaic hell is situated at the end of the Transiberian Railroad, but it is said in whispers only; Soviet espionage is everywhere, and the ancient, simple Mongol loyalty has become a thing of the past.

The Panshan Lama, the Pontiff of the Lamaic Buddhists, has only recently begun to express himself on Bolshevism, after having been reticent for a long period. He has abandoned his former real or assumed indifference and has declared that " Bolshevism is the enemy of Buddhism." He lives now in Peking, in one of the Pavillons of the Forbidden City. Hundreds of Mongols come to him daily to receive his instructions. However, these instructions, owing to racial and religious reasons, cannot envisage more than passive resistance, not active opposition.

Diplomats may find explanations and excuses for these violations of Chinese sovereignty and of ancient Mongol autonomies, for the demoralization of a race and a country which only yesterday was a delightful example of old patriarchal virtues. But only the weak government of a divided country, like China, could pretend to believe the verbal assurances which Moscow is offering it.

There are, however, certain features — accessory perhaps — which it does not seem the Chinese can pretend to ignore, alive as they always are to matters of form. There exists an official Russian publication which can be bought in Moscow for a few kopeks. It is the " Diplomatic Annual of the U.S.S.R." If one opens it at the letter M, one finds in the list of sovereign foreign states with full diplomatic representation, right after Mexico, this other new nation: *Mongolia*. There follows the name of the " Ambassador " of the U.S.S.R. (the Soviety have adopted a single title, Ambassador, in their internal administrative organization for the heads of all their diplomatic missions; it is only abroad that these heads assume one of the old titles, Minister or Ambassador). After the name of the Ambassador to Mongolia come the names of his numerous secretaries and attachés.

Masters as they are in the art of propaganda, the Bolshevik agents in China, assisted by the cowardice and vanity of the Chinese Government, have been successful in enforcing a complete silence as to their actions in Mongolia. The verbal campaign of the

Chinese against the " unequal treaties," was very useful in this respect, and the Russians at once saw the twofold advantage to be gained by it.

It was also under cover of this campaign that Russia was able quietly to increase her influence in Northern Manchuria by means of that powerful arm, the Chinese Eastern Railway.

Anyone interested in the Far East knows the present condition of this railroad. This is it, in a few words: The Chinese Eastern Railway crosses the northern part of Manchuria, linking Siberia to Vladivostok, now Russian territory, although up till 1860 it had belonged to China. Harbin, the great new city of the Far East, which has begun to rival Shanghai as a pleasure center, is in the middle of this line; it is the seat of the administration of the Chinese Eastern Railway with its hundreds of Russian officials, great and small. It is from Harbin that a line branches off to Dairen and Port-Arthur. Only one-third of this branch-line, from Harbin to Changchun, at present belongs to the Chinese Eastern Railway; the other two-thirds passed to Japan after the treaty of Portsmouth which in 1905 ended the Russo-Japanese War; it is run in a most efficient manner by the South Manchurian Railway.

It should be remembered that the old Trans-Manchurian Railway never did belong to the Russian Government, but was the property of a company constituted according to Russian law but receiving its seal from the Chinese Government, which means that it was a Chinese concern. The President of the Company had to be appointed by the Chinese Government and ownership of the shares was restricted to Chinese and Russian subjects, governments and official bodies being excluded. As there was not sufficient capital to build the railway, the money was borrowed from the Russian Government and stock was given them as security. The Russian Government was not the owner, but simply a creditor, a distinction which has been frequently overlooked.

In 1924 the Chinese Government recognized Soviet Russia. The two Governments agreed that they ought to take over the Chinese Eastern Railway, without compensation of any kind to the Company. Among the dispossessed creditors are several capitalists of Western Europe and the United States. So far as I know, no representations on this subject have ever been made to Moscow.

It remains to this day a complete mystery what reasons — if indeed there be any honorable ones — prompted the Chinese Government to accept this arrangement. For these are its real results, which make it neither more nor less than one of the " unequal treaties " against which the Chinese are waging their noisy campaign:

1. The Sovietic Government acquired the right to operate outright a railway on Chinese territory with-

out any form of reciprocity for the Chinese Government, and in spite of the fact that no analogous case exists elsewhere in China.

2. The Sovietic Government consequently acquired a privilege not enjoyed by any other foreign government in China, which is contrary to the principles laid down by the Washington Conference.

3. This privilege virtually makes a zone of Russian influence from Manchuly (Russo-Chinese frontier) to Changchun.

4. This zone of influence is detrimental to other foreign interests, as American oil companies are prepared to testify, and as preferential tariffs in favor of Russian oil companies prove.

5. All officials and workmen on the Chinese Eastern Railway must be Russians or Chinese which is in violation of the principle of equal opportunities.

6. All these officials and workmen are obliged to belong to Syndical Unions under strict control of the Soviet Executive Center of the Syndical Union in Moscow. This means that thousands of people on Chinese territory, and often Chinese subjects, have blindly to obey the orders of a foreign government, and ironically enough it is the very government which most publicly renounced its extra-territorial rights. This state of affairs enables us to discover that, as far as extra-territoriality is concerned, the Russians today are better off than the Germans because every Russian

190

in China today is an official of some kind, except in Manchuria; and there they are under the " protection " of Sovietic institutions even more surely than in the old days of foreign privileges and consular tribunals. True that White Russians exist by the thousands in Shanghai, where they are reduced to the lowest forms of labor; but they no longer look upon themselves as Russians, and it is only to be expected that Moscow should completely disinterest itself from their fate.

7. Last but not least, the control of the vast revenues of the Chinese Eastern Railway remains exclusively in Sovietic hands. Not a cent of the approximatively twelve-million-dollar average yearly profit of the railway is administered or even seen by the Chinese, which, of course, gives the Russians strong administrative and political advantages.

Personally, I have never believed the tales of the huge sums of money flowing from Moscow to Peking or Canton for Bolshevik propaganda. But I am quite ready to admit that, controlled as it is by the Sovietic Government, a certain proportion of the revenues of the Chinese Eastern Railway may have been diverted to Bolshevik propaganda in China.

The legend of a constant pouring for years past of Bolshevik rubles into China has been especially propagated by the British communities in Shanghai and Tientsin.

Why?

The old powerful British merchants were seeing their financial situation shattered, they had been accustomed for decades to easy big gains and to a leisurely life, they lacked the courage to change their systems altogether: and their propaganda was an idea with an object. The object was to have the Powers — or England at least — hit at China under a pretense of fighting a Bolshevism which had never existed there. It is probable that present unruly China deserves a great many uncomplimentary epithets; but when the Englishmen of China chose the name " filobolshevik " it was because they wanted to give a dog a bad name and hang him.

Psychologically speaking, it is very strange that while all the yellow British press has been daily busy discovering and exploiting, for years, Bolshevik plots against pure, innocent Europe, scarcely a word has ever been said about the Russian infringements of Chinese sovereignty in Manchuria and Mongolia.

In a friendly talk with an old Chinese Prime Minister — now retired from public life, and with whose Confucian wisdom I kept company for two pleasant days in Dairen — I expressed to him my surprise at the silence maintained about imperialistic Russian advances in China.

" It may be " — so he answered me after a silence — " that your Western Governments do not care to expose to the hatred of our people a policy which is nothing but a unilateral application of the old policy of the zones of influence; for it is this policy that is dear to their hearts, and probably they would wish for nothing better than to be able to adopt it again, each one in his own interest, as Russia is doing now."

"No, no," I replied. "You pay too much honor to their poor Machiavellism. I am afraid that a much simpler explanation is nearer the truth. This explanation is: mental insufficiency; like the Austrian generals against the armies of the French Revolution, our diplomacy is still surprised and bewildered *vis-à-vis* with a new adversary armed with new methods, like Bolshevik Russia."

The phrase of the wise and old Chinese statesman proves, however, that even this man, Confucian at heart, rich, an exile after the Kuomintang success and therefore not sympathetic to the new ideas, shares with students, peasants, merchants, the contempt for, and hatred of, all foreigners.

This is the growing feeling in China. Russia, be she Red or White, is hated as much as we are hated. But with the two faces she is able to assume there, she knows better than we do how to further her traditional schemes. Stalin's Red emissaries march sometimes in China, perhaps unconsciously, in the footprints of the old czaristic generals and ambassadors. It is a moral and historical lesson.

XII

THE TURKISH DICTATORSHIP

O<small>NLY</small> one of the post-war dictators, Mustafa Kemal, appears to have been a success, up to the present at least.

It is worth while to find out the main reasons of this unique exception.

They will, I believe, be found in two orders of facts: that the rise of a real Turkish patriotism was a genuine happening, devoid entirely of the artificial characteristics of other nationalistic movements, and that it coincided with the beginnings of Kemal's political power; that Kemal, once in power, and even after his victories, remained faithful to the policy he had initiated under my very eyes, a policy of complete renunciation of any Osmanli idea of domination over non-Turkish peoples.

To realize these two facts is to grasp the main reason of Kemal's success.

Everybody knows that the Ottoman Empire had begun as the very opposite of a national state. It had not even a national name: Ottoman being simply the

195

European transformation of Osman, the name of the Prince who first brought his tribes to power and glory. Osman and his tribes were Turks, of course; but their other Turkish neighbors were probably hated by them more than the Christians who, in the west, became their best tax-payers, and the Albanians and Bosnians who kept their own language even when converted by the Osmanlis to the Moslem faith. It was only during the 19th century, when Greece, and after her the Balkan provinces — Serbia, Rumania, Bulgaria — broke away from Stambul that Anatolia became more and more the safest place of the Osmanli empire. The same Sultans who had lost the Rumelian conquests of their ancestors succeeded in the 19th century in curbing the feudal resistance of the Kurdistan clans and the individualistic independence of the Anatolian tribes. The " Turkification " of the Osmanli empire was prepared by the creation of the modern Turkish army organized on the Western basis of conscription from the civil population, to replace the Janissaries — a hereditary professional army of forced Christian converts — destroyed in 1826. The conscripts were nominally drawn from the whole Moslem population of the empire; but, practically, the toughest soldiers were supplied by the Anatolian peasantry, while the Anatolian upper classes ended by giving most of the officers and officials of the increasingly centralized empire.

When a conscious Turkish national movement be-gan, the Ottoman state was already resting on a practical foundation of Turkish nationality — which had never been during its great days of the 17th and 18th centuries. Only a Turkish soul was lacking. Even the Turks of Anatolia were still thinking of themselves in a catholic way with hardly a national complex; just as it was with the Western European nations before the 16th century.

As almost always happens, the political movement was preceded by a literary one, the origin of which must be sought in the humiliation all the Turks had felt when Austria-Hungary suddenly decided upon the annexation of Bosnia-Herzegovina. The " Pure Turkish " literary campaign was started in Salonika, in 1909, by a Turk of Diarbekir, a certain Zia boy. That Zia was from Diarbekir, a little Turkish enclave surrounded by Kurdish and Armenian zones, is a new proof that ardent nationalists often come from debatable borderlands. Zia's group started a campaign to purify the language, to oust all words of Arab and Persian origin and even — which seemed then an act of folly — to have the Koran translated from the Arab language into Turkish and to remove all Arab texts from the walls of the mosques. The disasters of the Balkan wars of 1912 and 1913 made " Pure Turkish " and Pan-Turanianism a practical aim in political life. Wide circles which had not been affected by

197

a purely literary movement felt the necessity of a national regeneration. Hundreds of societies were founded in Anatolia to promote education, emancipation of women, laicization of schools.

The greatest Eastern blunder of the Entente and of Wilson — the authorization granted to the Greeks to land at Smyrna in May 1919 — did the rest.

The landing of the Greeks was what, from Constantinople, where I had been sent as High Commissioner after the Armistice of October 30, 1918, I vainly advised the Big Four it would be: a bloody operation whence would issue wounded to death the very party whose violence could seem successful only to those who did not know how to see through appearances. Indeed, Greece was doomed on the very day Athens went mad with patriotic joy at the news that the Hellenic flag had been planted on the walls of Smyrna.

Mustafa Kemal, a general who had fought valiantly at the Dardanelles during the World War, and who had become very popular among his countrymen, was near Samsun, in Anatolia, when the news of the occupation of Smyrna reached him. As a very young officer, in 1908, he had already taken part as chief of the general staff of Mahmud Pasha in the march of the Macedonian troops on Constantinople, a march which resulted in forcing the Sultan Abdul-Hamid to grant a constitution — the beginning of the Young Turkish era.

Kemal, who has a born gift of eloquence and who had learned in 1908 how to use it with regiments not yet decided to march against the Padisha, decided in Samsun, alone, that Turkey should withstand Greece and, if needs was, the Entente. In the main Samsun mosque, he made a memorable speech to the numerous faithful assembled there, a speech which spread from mouth to mouth and town to town, with the characteristic swiftness of news-spreading in the East, and which everywhere caused a deep commotion. Invited by the Sultan — who, in Constantinople had become a mere puppet in the hands of the Entente — to come back at once to the capital, he went even further away from it; he went to Erzerum, on a tour of military inspection; in reality again a rebel against the Sultan, as in 1908.

The story is known.

A few months later he raised armed bands. And, under cover of these, he began to organize a serious army. The stronger he grew, the more Turks turned to him. The very officials of the Sublime Porte, while smiling and bowing to High Commissioners and Allied Generals in Constantinople, longed in their hearts for his triumph. To the Turks the end was henceforth plain. It was only a question of time. One point only remained uncertain: the decision of the Allies who, in April 1920, at the Inter-allied San Remo conference, had finally accepted the hard peace-terms drawn up by the British Government. On the eve of San Remo, in March, Lord Curzon said: " The effective strength of Kemal has been overestimated; he is not as important a factor as some assert " — and, by this general word " some " he referred to me who, now in Rome, continued to advocate a policy of peace with Turkey. Even more buoyantly in June, after San Remo, Lloyd George declared in a solemn speech in London, that Greece alone was capable of " taking the place " of the Ottoman Government.

At the following Inter-allied conferences at Boulogne, Spa and London (1920 and 1921), I alone never ceased to warn Lloyd George and Venizelos against the dangers of an Anatolian military invasion. If it were desired — I said and repeated and had it put on record — to intensify the life and strength of Turkish militarism and xenophobia the Lloyd Georgian schemes were certainly the best way of doing it.

In vain.

The die was cast, and Venizelos had his war, unfortunately for the Hellenic nation.

Beaten at first, the Greeks succeeded in the Summer of 1921 in occupying Afium-Karahissar and Kutaya. Their front held firm for a year; or, to be more exact, Kemal had the courage to wait — a courage rarer than the courage to attack — and to compel others to wait with him. Finally, when he felt that he

was ready, he struck a decisive blow. On August 26,
1922, he attacked south of Afium-Karahissar; on the
following day, the Greek lines were broken. The
Greek Commander-in-Chief, Tricupis, ordered a retreat that soon became a rout; on September 2nd
Tricupis himself was captured by a Turkish cavalry
squadron. The Turks occupied Smyrna one week
later. King Constantine lost his throne. And on October 11th — after Great Britain, France and Italy
had interposed between Turks and Greeks — we had
the final results of four years of blunders, illusions and excessive pretensions—the Armistice of
Mudania, by which Europe consented to the re-entry
into Constantinople and Eastern Thrace of the Ankara
Government; in short, to the triumphant return of the
Turks into Europe, under the leadership of the same
Mustafa Kemal whom, at the beginning of 1919, the
British agents in Constantinople had planned to arrest
and confine in Malta.

These details needed being recalled, since there
lies — in the foreign attempts after the armistice to
destroy the Turkish nation — the main explanation of
Mustafa Kemal's initial success as a leader.

But if Kemal's dictatorship still is, or still seems
to be a success after years of personal rule, the essential reason for it must be found in the fact that his
whole policy was marked by two rare decisions which

are the very opposite of what all dictators have always done and still do. Dictators always end in disaster because they are obliged to embark upon a policy of show and vain prestige; they have to supply " glory " to compensate for liberty. Kemal had the pluck and the originality to adopt a courageous line of renunciation at the beginning of his domination, and — what is still more original — to stick to it even amid the intoxication of military success.

The Turkish Empire, with its Caliphate, its threats of Jihad (Holy War), pretended to a world policy that had long been anachronistic. Kemal was the first to insist, at Ankara, that New Turkey must renounce all claims to influence outside her racial frontiers. Determined to remain the master in Turkey, he boldly abdicated all claims outside it. From the very first months of 1919 — I have already said that I was then in Constantinople as High Commissioner — I had proof that he had felt that there lay the only way to salvation for a really independent Turkey.

The head of the powerful Moslem sect of the Senussis, whose headquarters lay in the southern part of the Italian colony of Cyrenaica, had escaped to Brusa, in Asia Minor. Convinced as I was — and am — that only a policy of local autonomy and peace will give prosperity to our African colonies, I entered upon patient and lengthy parleys with the Senussi chief, offering to reinstate him in his possessions and to grant him a large share of autonomy if he would loyally and formally acknowledge the suzerainty of Italy and would bind himself to further our political and economic interests in Bengasi and Tripoli. The conversations were successful and led to a settlement which worked to our satisfaction until it was destroyed by the Fascist Government when it discovered in Cyrenaica a field for cheap and deceptive military successes. Anxious as I was to secure for Italy the allegiance of the Senussis, and fearing lest the Turks, whose defeat I knew to be apparent only, would influence them in the opposite direction, I gave some hint of my negotiations to Mustafa Kemal and his friends. They sent me the following answer: " The maintenance of Turkish domination over the Arabs has been one of the causes of our decline. We do not want to hear any more about them. Let them settle matters with you as they please, and as you please."

The courage of this answer confirmed me in my belief in Turkish awakening. And it goes to the credit of Kemal's statesmanship that he has never changed his mind on this question.

He had realized that imperial Turkey was a backward country between Europe and Asia; and that, by turning into a mainly Anatolian power, republican Turkey might become a factor for progress only if she looked upon central Asia as she does now. These are the real political innovations that Kemal has had the courage to devise and to carry out. That is why they are so little spoken of, and the world has eyes only for his minor and doubtful games of alphabetical and sartorial reforms.

It is worth while to bring out the fact that if this dictator seems, alone of his kind, to achieve success, it is because he has dared to do what no dictatorship has ever done — to cut down, or renounce, the noisy and rhetorical legacies which the empty prestige policy of the previous régime had bequeathed to him.

There is another thing that may be said in Kemal's favor and in his favor alone: By keeping patriotism one of the sacred forces of the nation — and not bringing it to the fever point and the verbal exaggerations one witnesses in certain Western European countries — Kemal may be sure that there will not be a crisis of patriotism in Turkey.

Unfortunately I am not so sure of that for the countries where the masses have witnessed the blasphemous attempts to identify a régime, a party, a faction with the most sacred emblems of the nation.

The field in which Kemal's errors probably have no redeeming point is that where he believed he might force the laws of economic life. Suspicion of Greeks and Armenians, who used in old Turkey to have the monopoly of commercial life, explains, but does not excuse, the fact that Kemal's policy has so blandly ignored all considerations of social economy.

Mustafa Kemal believed at the beginning of his government that it was enough to expel the foreigners from their jobs, to have all gains going into Turkish pockets. He had overlooked the fact that the mercantile genius of the Greeks, the Armenians and of all the Levantines of European origin had been created by centuries of tradition and work.

In reality, even the institutions which, in the past, naturally enough, had wounded Turkish pride, like the Public Debt Administration, had been for decades an asset to the Turks. It was indeed the *Dette Publique* (managed by Franco-British directors but with a staff including also Italians, Germans, etc.) which had developed silk, salt, tobacco industries, fisheries — all revenues assigned to it.

Ankara xenophobia has cost the Turks dear in the economic field.

True that we, Westerners, have paid the penalty for teaching the Turks, through an experience generations long, that our financial assistance almost always led to foreign political interference.

And this, all the Turks, Kemal no more than the others, are decided never again to admit.

In all fairness to Kemal and the Turks, it should not be forgotten, on the other hand, that the expulsion from Anatolia of all the rich and intelligent Hellenic colonies that for long centuries had kept in Western Asia the monopoly of trade, navigation, industry, was conceived by Venizelos under the form of a project for the exchange of populations. The Greek statesman had advocated this project several times from 1913 onwards. When a convention was signed in Lausanne on January 30, 1923, providing the compulsory exchange of national and religious minorities between Greece and Turkey, Venizelos must have known — he, the inventor of the idea and the ultimate maker of the Lausanne treaty — that the Turks would ruthlessly enforce all its clauses. It would have been impossible for them to do otherwise. A million and a half Asiatic Greeks, yesterday rich and happy, were cast back upon the coast of Hellas as pariahs. That such an event, worthy to rank with the barbarian migrations of the third and fourth centuries can have taken place without arousing the horror of the whole world is one of the main proofs of the mental disease and moral degeneracy that the war has left behind. Convinced as I am that Turkey lost by the exchange, as she has lost by all her xenophobia which was even applied to the commercial field, it was impossible to expect that Kemal and his Government would give up this unique chance of changing their country into a homogeneous Turkish State, containing, now, fewer extraneous elements than any other nation in Asia and probably even in Europe. But the responsibility for the

206

event must be left entirely with the man who first, and rashly, launched the idea of it, an idea which went counter to the very essence of the history of Anatolia.

What are the real feelings of the Turks towards Kemal's dictatorship.

The Turks — practically all the Turks — admit that the Osmanli dynasty was doomed; and that a republic was the only natural sequel.

It had been said and repeated by dozens of historians and orientalists that the Turks, as, by the way, the Russians, were deeply attached to their religious creeds. Experience has shown that this was little more than an appearance. After all, what Kemal dared to do against the Moslem religion would not have been enough to destroy a strong national religious feeling — granted that it existed. He closed the Sheri courts, the Dervish Tekehs and all other sorts of theological seminaries; he expelled the Khalif. But all that had been done in England by Henry VIII in the 16th century; and, in a way, in Italy in the 14th. Neither nation showed a decrease of religious zeal. Now, in Turkey, the mosques are empty; even in holy Brusa, in Asia Minor, the green-turbaned Imans deplore the growing indifference of their fellow-citizens. Enough to show that the Turks are apt to accept new situations quickly.

What has probably been favorable to Kemal in

207

their hearts is the fact that he has stuck to all the external forms of a republican democracy.

Only those who, like myself, have spent years in various Oriental capitals, know that, of all those nations which we — rightly or wrongly, probably wrongly — call backward, the Turks are the people most essentially democratic. Democratic they were even under the rule of the most despotic of their Osmanli sultans. It was old Ferid Pasha, Grand Vizier when I was *Chargé d'Affaires* in Turkey, who told me the story of the peasant from Konia who came to Stambul and went to the old Serai to see the Sultan and have a wrong redressed. Freely he arrived before the Divan where the Sultan was sitting among his ministers. And the old peasant simply asked: — *Khanghiniz Khunkiar?* (which of you is the Sultan?)

The Turks feel, with the instinct which rarely fails the Orientals, that Kemal's is an involuntary dictatorship — a dictatorship (I should dare to say) aiming at making autocrats and dictators impossible in the self-government of a renovated free nation.

Kemal's only error — like cne of the old autocrats whom he most resembles, Peter the Great — is to think too optimistically about the possibility of forcing the course of history.

Bibliography

Sforza, Count C. — *Diplomatic Europe Since the Treaty of Versailles.* — New Haven, Yale University Press, 1927.

Sforza, Count C. — *Makers of Modern Europe.* — Indianapolis, Bobbs Merrill, 1930.

Toynbee, A. J., and Kirkwood, K. P. — *Turkey.* — New York, Scribner's, 1927.

Waugh, Sir T. — *Turkey, Yesterday, Today and Tomorrow.* — London, Chapman, 1931.

XIII

THE SPANISH DICTATORSHIP

THE Spanish Dictatorship was born wholly in the shade of royal power.

No war-made officers unwilling to fall back to the gloom of their previous little jobs — as in Italy.

No *gentry* rushing to carry the strongholds of power by storm — as in Hungary.

Everything in Spain came from the center: the King and, with the King, the two great old régime forces — the Church, the Army — on which he deliberately chose to lean during the whole of his reign, blind to the warnings which loyal Spaniards, like Romanones or Calanejas, did not spare him, hoping as they did that he would understand that his interest lay in identifying his power and his name with a policy of social progress.

The Spanish Dictatorship that was, had not even the excuse of having been bound up with a social and economic crisis of the country.

Being an essentially artificial fact, when the dictatorship crashed, all it schemed and did fell with it.

A few months later, in 1931, the monarchy followed in its fall. And the responsibilities, and the trial of the dynasty have obliterated from men's minds the remembrance of that last episode of the royal policy: the dictatorship of Primo de Rivera.

If the last chapter but one of this book is dedicated to the Spanish dictatorship, it is not because of any desire of rounding off a formal geography of dictatorial Europe. At that rate, one could omit it.

The pages which follow have another aim. They purport to show, synthetically, the analogies between the end of the Spanish Dictatorship and what will probably be the end of other dictatorships; and also, and chiefly, to show how the Spanish Dictatorship differed essentially from all the others; that is, in the fact that it was willed by the King who thought to find a shelter for personal errors of his where he soon found his undoing.

The sudden end of the Spanish Dictatorship surprised world opinion when almost all the newspapers of America and Europe were still printing headlines of this kind: *All Spain for Rivera's Rule* or *Spain Finances Prosper* or *Amazing Progress in Spain,* and so on.

Almost without transition these newspapers were obliged, faced with facts, to admit that the whole scaffolding of Spanish prosperity and of Spanish well-

211

being had crumbled to bits; and that poor Rivera's cleverest achievement had been to die before he was thrown in prison.

Since Primo de Rivera's dictatorship was extolled for years in the main newspapers of the world for the marvelous awakening of Spanish economy, one thing only is worth noting here, where we have dealt solely with dictatorships still living: to prove that the Spanish dictator falsified the budget for years.

I wish to limit myself to those figures which were published after the fall of de Rivera, but whilst he was still alive; he might have tried to contradict them; he did not dare; he knew that it was impossible:

A. *Effective Revenue of the State:*
1921–22 (last of Liberal
   Government)   Pesetas: 2,331,874,251
1929   "   3,724,000,000

B. *Expenditure of the State:*
1921–22   Pesetas: 3,435,331,557
1929   "   4,718,600,000

C. *Debts of the State:*
1922   Pesetas: 14,435,663,063
1929   "   20,182,457,118

D. *Debts of the Municipalities:*

1921	Pesetas:	565,150,939
1929	"	1,618,384,065

E. *Debts of the Provinces:*

1921	Pesetas:	72,424,725
1929	"	318,350,340

F. *State Debts with Foreign Banks:*

1921		nil
1929: Morgan & Co.	Dollars:	20,000,000
Midland Bank	"	37,900,000
Rothschild	"	9,700,000

Total: Dollars: 67,600,000

The result ascertained for the Spanish Dictatorship will perhaps constitute a rehearsal of what will prove to be the truth for other dictatorships. Hence its moral value.

That is why it would not be surprising if, when new denouements come, public opinion, opening its eyes too late, will look for the reason of so much press laudation at the doors of those foreign banks which for years took an interest in their debtors — the dictatorships — such as they never felt in free non-indebted democracies.

Probably, ultimate results will be even worse for

213

other dictatorships. For, now that the whole world has not a word of appreciation left for Primo de Rivera's régime, it is only fair to acknowledge one merit in the man; one only, but a singular one.

Being a Spanish general, being the embodiment of the old Spanish army of the 19th century, the army of the *pronunciamientos;* having shown, in the problems of civil life, the incurable *naïveté* of soldiers who believe that problems are arduous only "because civilians do not know how to exact obedience," Primo de Rivera however, did understand that, in Morocco, his King, his army colleagues, all those who had wished to play the *conquistadores* there, were wrong. As a very young general (a young general through nepotism, being the nephew of a famous general who got him rapid promotions), Primo de Rivera had even gone so far as to write in favor of a cession to England of the Spanish possessions in Morocco, as an exchange for Gibraltar. In spite of his supporters of the army, one thing he grasped after a few months of office: that the Moroccan adventure was eating up the resources and the very life of Spain. He determined to force a policy of withdrawal upon the army. A fact even rarer, he decided to apply his policy in person, and went to Morocco where he conducted the retreat. Since that time, the Spanish zone of Morocco has kept quiet, and the Spanish budget was saved considerable expenditure.

No other dictator, with the exception of Mustafa Kemal, has dared to carry out a policy which went counter to the traditions of external prestige and of militarism.

Primo de Rivera did. He knew the question: it was even the only question he did know; and therein he rendered a service to his country, despite the King, despite the army.

But his mistakes and misapprehensions in all other fields were sufficient to ruin the country.

I have said that the Spanish dictatorship has been the unique case of a dictator created, invented, by the sovereign of a monarchical country.

Alfonso XIII's experiment in vicarious dictatorship had a reason — a personal one. Even the best friends of the ex-King have found it impossible validly to deny that the reason why the King suppressed constitutional government in 1923 was his supreme personal interest in preventing a real investigation of the tragedy of the Morocco campaign, where many thousands of brave Spaniards lost their lives. Responsibility for the *débâcle* and for the slaughter had been traced to Alfonso himself. He wanted Morocco's war to be his war — as another Spaniard, Empress Eugénie, thought that the Franco-Prussian war would be *sa guerre*. He wanted rapid success, and he was foolish enough to send secret encouragement for im-

mediate military action to General Silvestre, chief of
the Melilla division, who wanted to strike a blow at
the Moroccans, and to destroy, in that way, the wise
policy of peaceful understanding with the tribes that
his superior, General Berenguer, had inaugurated.
Berenguer's policy had already won to Spain great
moral and territorial advantages, and at a very modest
cost of blood and money. But one thing was suffering
from this wise policy: the promotions and the prestige
of the officers.

Encouraged by the King, keeping his military chief
Berenguer in the dark, the gallant Silvestre dashed
into a dangerous position, where he suffered a terrible
defeat. In one day Spain lost all the territory she had
won in years; the dead, wounded and prisoners
amounted to thousands.

Silvestre committed suicide.

But everybody in Spain began to whisper about
the King's direct responsibilities. The disaster, indeed,
had been his work.

Faced with a national scandal — a parliamentary
inquiry seeming imminent — he probably felt that
his chances of pulling through would be very slender.
Vain more than proud, he staved off a reckoning with
his people for nearly eight years by hiding himself behind the dictator invented by him, Primo de
Rivera.

The personal character of this Bourbon — perhaps

the last of this millenary family to have sat on a throne — is the key to his political errors which finally cost him his crown.

The enemies of Alfonso XIII have compared him to his ancestor Ferdinand VII, the treacherous and cowardly king of Napoleonic times. Alfonso has been much better than his ancestor who kotowed to Bonaparte as long as the Corsican was strong and who, when the Spaniards reconquered him a throne, came back surrounded by a *camarilla* of the most despicable courtiers.

The comparison seems highly unfair in many ways. It cannot be denied, however, that Alfonso, intelligent, or at least quick in a Kaiser Wilhelm way, has committed the terrible error of believing that a king has the right to deceive his councilors. Base astuteness he believed to be diplomatic skill. He reminds me more of another of the Spanish kings, Ferdinand of Aragona, the conqueror of Granada, who having been told that the king of France had complained that he, Ferdinand, had deceived him twice, answered at once triumphantly:

" No, no, it is a lie. I have deceived him ten times."

Only in one general sense, Alfonso is more like Ferdinand VII than like the Aragonese. Ferdinand VII was, like Alfonso, a descendant of the Bourbon line created in Spain by Philip of Anjou, Louis XIV's grandson. The Frenchman brought into Spain the

secret law of the French monarchy after Louis XIV:
" *Tel est nostre bon plaisir.*" And that is what Alfonso
always believed.

Like William II — whom he resembles mentally
although lacking all the pseudo-Lohengrinian stuff
which was such a large part of the make-up of
the Hohenzollern — Alfonso showed, as soon as
he ascended the throne, that he would not suffer
his authority being put in a prudent shade. Count
Romanones, who as a Cabinet Minister assisted at
both the King's abdication and the first Cabinet
Council held by him a few hours after he had sworn
in the Cortes to "observe the Constitution," on
May 17, 1902, described the latter scene a few years
ago:

"The King, as if he had never done anything else
but preside over Cabinet meetings all his life, with
great coolness and an imperious voice, at once addressed the War Secretary and submitted him to a
close examination with regard to the causes of a recent
decree shutting down the military colleges. Ample
explanations,[1] ample for his wonted laconicism, were
given by General Weyler, but Don Alfonso was not
satisfied and held that the colleges should be re-
opened. Weyler replied with respectful firmness; but,
when the argument was taking a dangerous turn, Sa-

[1] Excess of officers as a result of the end of the Spanish-
American war.

218

gasta [2] cut in adopting the King's view and thereby defeating the War Secretary.

"After a brief pause, the young King, with the text of the Constitution in his hand, read paragraph 8 of Article 55,[3] and he added, by way of comment:

"' As you have heard, the Constitution confers upon me the granting of titles and grandeeships; and I warn you that I reserve for myself entirely the exercise of this right.'

"We heard these words with great surprise. The Duke of Veragua, a scion of one of our most illustrious families [4] and a man of decided Liberal spirit, met the King's words with a single reply; by reading Article 49 of the Constitution which said: ' No order of the King can be put into operation unless it be countersigned by a minister.'

"But Sagasta did not attach importance to honors and decorations and did not intervene. Therefore the lesson was lost."

Such were the beginnings of Alfonso's reign: personal power, protection of the army against the interests of the country, importance given to the instruments of royal favor among the privileged classes.

But what lost him more than anything else was: his

[2] Sagasta was the Prime Minister and had been for many years the leader of the Liberal Party.

[3] " The King makes all appointments to civil posts and grants honors and distinctions of all kinds."

[4] The Veraguas are the direct descendants of Columbus.

naïve conviction that he was the master (and this might have looked royal); his desire to be always in the limelight, which was less royal and more theatrical, — just as with the German Kaiser with whom he never got on, for two actors of the same style never love one another.

When before the War I used to see in Vienna the old Austrian emperor, Francis Joseph, I often thought of him as the last of the sovereigns — and so he was in his own mind. As a young diplomat attached in 1910 for a few months to the Italian Foreign Office, I saw Theodore Roosevelt rather frequently during his visit to Italy; from him I heard that Francis Joseph had frankly admitted to Roosevelt during his Vienna days that he was in fact the last monarch left in Europe.

In reality there was one other monarch in Europe who shared with Francis Joseph the conviction that " My subjects are my subjects by God's will and my quality of King makes me a man apart." This man was Alfonso XIII. Born a king — the one sovereign in modern Europe actually born a king — he believed all his life — and probably he goes on believing in his exile — that through the proud Habsburg and Bourbon descent he has been invested with a superior right, that the kingdom over which he has reigned was his property, that the people who made it up were his people.

220

Compared to a belief so naïve, yet so strong, the boastful talk of pre-War Kaiser Wilhelm about his divine right was merely a proof that the Hohenzollern was not so certain of what he was advancing. He talked too much about it.

This much at best must be granted to Alfonso: that he was so certain of his supreme position that he almost never mentioned it, just as was the case with the only other authentic example of monarchical certainty — Francis Joseph.

But in one respect Alfonso has differed all his life from his Austrian " good brother." Francis Joseph was more of a real monarch than young Alfonso because he had never been guilty of that supreme act of a sovereign's bad taste — being brilliant. Francis Joseph was terribly boring all his life, and he knew that it was his right and his duty to be a bore. What the last Austrian Emperor felt by instinct, he became even more convinced of by experience. He saw that his ally, Wilhelm II, whom he disliked so cordially, was brilliant. Brilliant in a way was another sovereign whom he did not dislike, Edward VII. But the Austrian Emperor knew that these kinds of success were beneath his rank, and he despised them.

Sometimes events turned out to Alfonso's credit: was it not because of his rooted belief in his right to decide and rule that he dared to take steps that would have made others tremble — others certainly more intelligent than he? When he seemed strong it was because he was unable to see a far-off danger looming over him, the new energies slowly coming to life in the depths of the old Castilian nation.

Not only was he lacking in ponderation.

He also lacked another quality, at least as essential for a sovereign: the art of choosing friends and ministers.

William I of Prussia was a good man with an extremely mediocre intelligence. All the same he remains a great sovereign because, in spite of the thousands of little wounds inflicted thereby on his pride, he always kept a man of Bismarck's size in power — just as Victor Emmanuel did with Cavour in Italy.

But with Alfonso and his reign it has been even worse than choosing poor advisers when he felt free to do so. He went further, and any quacks who came forward claiming that they possessed marvelous formulae for trade, for industry or public works, were sure to find an easy admirer in the King. The quacks, through the strength of his support, frequently got monopolies and concessions. Gigantic graft invaded the country through them. And many in Spain believed, and still believe that part of the bribes went into Alfonso's pockets, which is false, I am sure.

But the thing that was wrong with the sovereign was something as bad: it was his childish, imprudent way to believe that he knew better, that he was omniscient, that he was infinitely above his ministers, his officials and his countrymen.

One must admit that it was difficult for Alfonso to be different. Has he not mixed in his blood the traditions and inheritances of the two most autocratic royal families — the Hapsburgs and the Bourbons?

But it was not worth while to have had one's self proclaimed for years the wariest man in Europe, and to fail to perceive the deep changes which were occurring in the Spanish soul; and that it was no longer sufficient, in order to reign, to give tokens of complicity to the Church and to the Army, two institutions which in Spain were more and more living upon themselves, cutting themselves off from everything saving their own, and immediate, interests.

Those who, until the spring of 1931, considered as permanent and immutable certain turns of mind and morals in Spain and optimistically concluded thence on behalf of Don Alfonso, were simply forgetting that various are the ways of being still monarchical.

If one of them is the blind reverence which was shown to kings and emperors in the Germany and Austria of yesterday, the Spaniards had another way. They had remained monarchists, but they had never given up their proud individualism. While we were still thinking only of the Spain of the *pronunciamientos,* the Spanish nation, recovered from the wastage of Catholic absolutism, was turning to the modern world, although in her own way.

For quite a few years, Don Alfonso had been the only monarchist of his own type in Spain. After all, according to the Spanish tradition, the nation alone had always been considered there as sovereign, the king being simply the agent of the people. This conception, which was embodied in the Constitution of 1876 that Alfonso violated and destroyed, has constantly been strong through all Spanish history, and it has always proved to be still alive even after long periods of sleep during absolutist Catholic rule. Back in the feudal twelfth century the members of the Cortes were taking the following oath of fealty to the king on entering their office: " We and you are equals, but we accept you as our king on condition that you obey the law." — Alfonso of Bourbon did not obey the law — and he had to go, in the end.

I do not like to bring too severe a judgment on a man who now must cruelly suffer, if he knows how to suffer.

But this must be said as a moral.

This king to whom American and European snobbery had given a reputation for quick intelligence and for chivalrous character, this man who believed that he was the most kingly king of all the kings who remain in Europe, proved not to have comprehension enough to understand that the monarchical principle is directly and essentially antagonistic to the dictatorial principle.

A monarchy rests on divine right, as it did in Austria, or on popular will, as it does in England. A dictatorship resting exclusively on material force is essentially anti-monarchical because it is against divine right just as it is against popular will.

Alfonso of Bourbon thought that to put Primo de Rivera in power as dictator would simply mean to get out of trouble. He did not realize that he was making of his monarchy an empty and useless frame.

Probably he does now. Too late.

Bibliography

Alba, S. — *L'Espagne et la Dictature.* — Paris, Valois, 1930.
Cambo, F. — *Les Dictatures.* — Paris, Alcan, 1930.
Madariaga, S. de. — *Spain.* — London, Benn, 1930.

XIV

CONCLUSIONS

ANALOGIES

T HE preceding pages have shown how the various European dictatorships differ in their origins and in their subsequent developments.

Those analogies — more evident and obvious — which may be drawn between them, are, for the most part, negatives; except in the case of Turkey, they are " ties of common funk " and hatred.

The essential link between, not only the dictatorships now in power, but between them and the dictatorial movements in France and Germany, is: a clouding — especially among the middle classes — of the Liberal and Democratic conscience, which had seemed a permanent conquest at the end of the 19th and beginning of the 20th centuries.

We are confronted with the same movement — more wide-spread, more complex, and more turbid — as that which seemed to sweep over Europe after the Napoleonic Wars; when the Holy Alliance for many years thought itself strong enough to drug and

to stifle the movement toward human freedom which
had begun at the end of the 18th century with the
American and French Revolutions; and that even the
military madness of the First Empire period had, in a
way, continued, because wherever Bonaparte passed,
there he destroyed the " *ancien régime* " institutions.
The very kings of his creating proved, from their
thrones, that Royalty was dead.

Of course, as history never repeats itself, the analogies between the anti-Liberal reaction of the Holy
Alliance and the varying forms of Fascist reaction,
are far from perfect. Above all, blind, selfish and
ungenerous as the 1815 reaction was, it only aimed
at the maintenance of outward order, and a formal
peace. Honest according to their lights, men of good
faith after their fashion, the Sovereigns of the Holy
Alliance, with their Metternichs and their Solaros
della Margherita, believed that the Revolution had
only been a passing disease, and that the " *bons peu-
ples* " would be only too delighted to fall back into
their old ruts. The dictators of after-war Europe,
many of them former demagogues, know better; that
is why their moral tyranny is far more invading and
suffocating. They would like to ferret among men's
consciences and to force their adherence; (hence, for
example, the official slogan in Fascist Italy: " He who
is indifferent is an enemy "). They go in terror of the
leaven of freedom which they know still to exist, ir-

227

repressible even in regions where they would seem to have spread silence and death.

ILLUSIONS

In order to bring a serene judgment to bear on the probable duration of these dictatorships, the psychological reactions which helped to give them birth must be divided into two different groups.

First, the War, with its immediate moral effects.

In 1914, '15 and '16, the war-cry of the Entente was " Freedom and Democracy." In 1917 and '18 came America's turn to hear herself say that the world must be made safe for Democracy. " To ensure Democracy " Americans went into the War. With Great Britain, France and Italy they won it.

And on this followed . . . a wave of autocracies and dictatorships.

Yet, was it not ever thus? In ancient Greece, where the Persian Wars produced Pericles and his long-drawn autocracy; in America, — may one say? — whose Revolution and whose wars did, truly, begin with a Jefferson, but ended with his most out-and-out antagonist, Hamilton.

We might almost wonder why, in Europe, things have not turned out worse than they have, after a war such as that of 1914–18, which surpassed all others in violence and in universality; a war which — often against the wish of those who preached it — became an open school of lies, calumnies and hatreds. On this subject I have already touched in the first chapter of this book.

Both in principle and in practice, Democracy was bound to suffer fatally from this, since Democracy is essentially rooted in mutual toleration. If England has become *Mater parlamentorum* it is because the classic phrase, "His Majesty's loyal Opposition," ended by actually representing the psychology and political manners of England.

During the four years of war, and the Shylockian months of the peace negotiations, no room was found for toleration, for mutual understanding. Did Caillaux and Malvy oppose the policy of the men in power? Jail and exile. Did Erzberger and Rathenau contemplate a peace detested by the Junkers? Assassinated. Did Bissolati speak to the Italians of a generous peace with Jugoslavia? Shouted down and persecuted as a traitor.

Dictatorships are no new expression of some new political thought, as those who profit from them, and the writers in their pay, would have us think. They are simply the natural continuance of the state of mind which war let loose. To make peace after four years of hatreds and massacres, by merely affixing a few signatures and seals to the foot of some parchment, would have been too tame an ending.

Yet we must admit the existence of another element, favorable to the birth of Dictatorships: I mean a certain dose of popular assent, either active or passive, at the moment of their formation.

Nothing more anti-historical than the way in which old Democratic historians described and describe dictatorships as dumbfounding, and fettering thro' sheer amazement, a population forcibly bereft of its political rights. Typical of this unreal romanticism is Victor Hugo's description and explanation of the happy stroke made by Louis Napoleon's *coup d'état,* while a foreigner, Marx, — a poet too, in his own way, — saw far more clearly how in 1851 and '52, one section of French public opinion gave way, while another was delighted.

Such toleration or satisfaction may either spring from disgust with a weak and incompetent government (as occurred in Italy with Facta in 1922); or else from irritation at long-continued and insensate agitations caused by demagogues, which was the case in Catalonia — (not without reason, when the Royal blow was struck to form a Dictatorship in Spain, did it first find adherents and material to hand in Catalonia).

Sometimes a paradox may appear: in the wish to find a " savior," coupled with their incapacity to generate him themselves, public opinion may range itself on the very side of the demagogue who has been whole-heartedly working for the destruction of law and order. It happened so with Caesar in Rome; for if the demagogy of the Gracchi had made the real autocracy of Sylla possible, that of an arch-demagogue, Caesar, brought about the founding of his own dictatorship as the cure for his demagogism. Such has been more than once the case.

It is more rare to find dictators who have succeeded because the ideas of which they made themselves protagonists were the ideas of the moment. This happened with Lenin. His power was due, not to his Marxist ideology, but to the fact that his actions brought about what practically the whole of Russia — Russia of the villages — wanted: Peace at any price, and the land for the peasant.

The Soviet régime, and its length of duration, will eventually be explained by this fact alone: That it was the instrument which achieved these two ends.

It is a far cry from this to the program of Italy, constantly shifting as if it were stage scenery; or the Polish program, sentimentally behind the times by some three or four generations. . . .

REALITIES

The spirit, and the spirit alone, it is which gives the breath of life to Revolutions, and directs the windings of a people's history.

Frederick II, the Hohenstaufen Emperor whose name rang through Italy and the Levant of the 13th century, left a far slighter trace behind him than his contemporary, Francis of Assisi. Charles V is a negligible figure compared with Martin Luther. During the Italian *Risorgimento*, Mazzini appeared to be worsted; but he left a message for future generations, and his name is still today a beacon light to a Europe who looks for her path.

For this reason, the Russian Revolution *is* a revolution; and would have remained one, even if the White Generals of 1920 and 1921 had succeeded in crushing it.

On the other hand, all those other dictatorships which have pompously proclaimed themselves to be Revolutions, only were, and only will remain, *coups d'état*.

— But some of these are still in being?

No matter! The *coup d'état* of Louis-Napoleon Bonaparte lasted many years, too; from 1852 to 1870. It never was more than a *coup d'état*. It disappeared at Sedan, in mud and blood. And, the day after, nothing was left; or, rather, there remained some great Paris *boulevards* (all dictatorships abound in public works), and, a heavy balance, an era of corruption which could only end as it did end — in war and defeat.

Even those dictatorships which are not born of fraud and comedy leave, in the long run, a heritage of political danger and moral lowering. This, even

232

when the Dictator himself was not lacking in elements of greatness.

I almost believe that the greatest factors in Germany's misfortunes were two persons — Bismarck and William II — the first having a much heavier responsibility than the second, as a great man must have in proportion to an amateur.

Had Bismarck really the greatness of a founder of nations?

A wide discussion on this point would probably be out of place, here. But I cannot hide the fact that, in my opinion — paradoxical or disrespectful as that may seem — he was the possessor of admirable diplomatic gifts, rather than that essential gift of a statesman — seeing into the future. The mere diplomat does not need this kind of genius; he works only for immediate results. And such — though I feel a certain hesitation in suggesting it, confronted as I am by a plebiscite of contrary opinions — seems to me to have been Bismarck's way of working.

Once only did he see far into history, but on that day he was in happy contradiction of his old habits. It was just after the Prussian victories over Austria in 1866, when, alone against his King, and, of course, against all the generals, he forced a peace which did not take an inch of territory from Austria. That very day he created the Triple Alliance, with which he won for decades German hegemony in Europe.

233

But, apart from this episode, what is the career of Bismarck but a series of errors, or miscalculations?

He did not seize the opportunity of creating a Colonial empire for Germany when it could be had for the asking. In this mistake are to be found the tardy violences of the post-Bismarckian German policy, with the interventions at Tangier, Agadir and so on — all those incidents which were the forerunners of the World War.

He fought the Catholic Church and made the Catholics into virtual enemies of the state; and in this way he embittered the situation in archi-Catholic Alsace-Lorraine; the result being that even now the Catholic center is one of the deciding parties in Germany.

He planned the destruction of the Polish element in the Reich; and the Poles of Posnania remained true to their Polish sentiments — both the landowners on their castles and the peasants in their villages.

He irritated the Alsatians, when a mild policy might have induced them to become more or less good Germans. By bullying them, he aroused their Celtic spirit, still alive under their German language. Fidelity to France was their answer to the bully.

If we examine with perfect objectivity the astounding episodes of Bismarck's career, we see that under all his immediate successes is hidden the fatal seed of sure future disaster. Strong and rare type of man as he was, he might have been more at home in the Crusades

234

or with the Spanish conquistadors. Confronted with modern living entities he was less at home. He knew how to destroy his opponents; but, after all, that is easy when one is in power and has no scruples, when one neither cares nor deigns to guess what is bound to follow.

To the political responsibilities of the titanic nineteenth-century German two may be added, of which only one is directly Bismarck's doing.

He reduced the Germans to a sort of mental servitude; he degraded them into experts (wise and clever as they may have been), without any desire or possibility of taking their share in political life. Personally he had the selfish excuse that his was a sort of genius, and daily events were masterfully treated by him while he remained in power.

But when William II — the weak, vain man — not content with his Imperial crown, became his own Chancellor, his subjects, who under Bismarck's iron rule had forgotten how to raise their heads, followed meekly behind their blind pastor.

Even today the shadow of the gigantic Chancellor is holding back his country in the road of conscious civic responsibility. Nothing is more disquieting for the future development of the German political mind than to see the quantities of books on Bismarck which are published each year — with none of them daring to call the hero to account. On the contrary, the Bismarckian cult seems sometimes a pretense or a prayer for the coming of the superman who might regain her former prestige for Germany.

Bonaparte, with all his military glories, set France on the path of a demographic decline. Bismarck sowed the seeds out of which came the recent German disasters.

Bismarck never believed in a free national effort; he made his own people — the people who had given Luther to the world, mentally the freest people in Europe — into a crowd of admiring merchants, who used to say: Our man of genius knows; let us be guided by him.

Bismarck had one excuse, and only one; as a statesman he felt embarrassed by certain natural tendencies of the German soul, and wanted to have them changed. There was an excess of romanticism which gave to the German inner spiritual life a sort of dangerous penchant for political inaction. And, like a hero of the old German Valhalla, he decided to call back his Teutons to a sense of practical life; he rallied them around a formula of concrete action, of material conquests, of organized obedience. He made a great Germany — but at the cost of the Germans. A second-rate contentment developed among those who had been a nation of thinkers.

Once in his life, I said, did Bismarck see far into the future; when he refused to take away even an inch of territory from vanquished Austria. One might add perhaps another moment in his life. It was in 1892, when, removed from power, he chose deliberately to deliver with elaborate éclat a speech to the students of the Jena University and told them that absolutism was a poison for the moral life of a nation, that to save Germany it was necessary to strengthen the force of Parliament and of public opinion.

But this vision came too late. Certain truths must be spoken by public men when they are in power, not when their words may seem a mere outburst from politicians furious at having been dismissed by their Sovereigns.

They may go on building their new aristocratic theory, the French gentlemen who have invented the so-called doctrine of Nationalism as opposed to the Liberal conception of life; but these hard facts remain: That the War was won by the peoples imbued with democratic traditions, and that the only autocratic state belonging to the democratic coalition — Russia — was the only one to fall to pieces. Germany, the only one of the great European states which had reached unity by military force, and by " *raison d'état,*" after despising and rejecting a previous opportunity of unification on a democratic basis — Germany alone, powerful as it was, showed itself in the days of trial far weaker than it had appeared to be. This, indeed, is not a party opinion, nor is it the opinion of former enemies. It is what is now openly recognized and admitted by many of the keenest thinkers of the German people.

The bitter experience of history is more eloquent than any philosophical, or pseudo-philosophical, generalization.

THE "GOOD DICTATOR"

Thus, even with a good Dictator, the nation is sooner or later bound to pay terrible penalties for having endured his rule, and for having ceased to uphold their political ideals, or even their political passions.

To any reader who might feel drawn to contend that " political passions " are frequently cumbersome and sterile things, I would leave Machiavelli to reply for me; not Machiavelli of " The Prince," whose " brutality " and " cynicism " Fascist writers admire, thinking that it suffices to make them into " *realpolitiker;* " [1] but the true, immortal Machiavelli of

[1] Almost pathetic in its mental simplicity is the tendency of persons of Fascist type — be they Black Shirts in Italy, Nazis in Germany, or Camelots du Roy in France — to admire a cheap Machiavelli invented by centuries of Catholic hatred and of Protestant cant. Because of this old foolish myth of a cynical Machiavelli, Rocco, Minister of Justice of the Fascist Government, wrote: " It is from Machiavelli that Fascism comes — both doctrine and action."

Probably the Fascist Minister of Justice meant the following passages of " The Prince ":

" He who intends to obtain supreme power must decide upon

the *Deche:* " Those who condemn the struggles . . . blame the things which were first causes of the freedom; they pay more attention to the noise . . . of these struggles than to their political results." [2]

---

the necessary cruelties and commit them at once. . . ." (Chap. VIII.)

" The security of conquest must be found in arming our own followers. . . ." (Chap. XX.)

" If the people do not believe in the Prince any more, he must make them believe in him by force." (Chap. VI.)

" A prudent Prince is not bound to keep his word, when the reasons that gave origin to his promise disappear." (Chap. XVIII.)

How distant, however, are these detached sentences from the real Machiavelli, as he reveals himself when studied in all his works, and especially in the most profound of them, the *" Deche."*

No one appears less Machiavellian than Machiavelli does there. In the *" Deche "* the philosopher's admiration is lavished on the great days of republican Rome, whose free government he preferred to any other.

If Machiavelli happened to make the grim statements of " The Prince," he did so because it is only the pure of heart who can say what is generally hidden by most men in the depths of their souls. " The Prince " was a serene survey of the political possibilities of the sixteenth century. It canot be understood, it cannot be judged, apart from the period that gave it birth.

There had been no great demonstrations, in Machiavelli's time, showing in what spirit a national moral unity may create lasting successes, such, for instance, as the action of France when faced by reactionary Europe, and of the Americans in their War of Independence.

Had Machiavelli witnessed a George Washington, he would probably have written another " Prince." He would have realized that what is necessary to create a great nation is not an individual will dominating a people (the two Bonapartes with the disasters they brought to France, as do all dictators in the

In the most favorable hypothesis, the nation under a good Dictator can only turn into a syndicate of egotists — nothing more.

It was the *imperators,* who were nothing else than permanent dictators, who atrophied every virtue of the *cives romani;* the patricians ceased to use their responsibilities, the plebeians were no longer able to furnish soldiers to the *res publica.*

Among modern Dictators, he who for many years seemed to be crowned with the most steady success was Porfirio Diaz, in Mexico.

When in Mexico, in the Spring of 1931, I was able to speak of that old despot with aged men who had known him, fought against him, foreseen his inevitable crash; but, being men of serene mind, they readily agreed with me that Diaz, like Bismarck, had possessed elements of greatness. Conscious of his own superiority, he was never — and in this respect he excelled Bismarck — jealous; and always raised those Mexicans who seemed to be of the highest caliber, to the highest offices; this he did with Liman-

long run, would have been a counterpart to his Borgia); he would have seen that what is paramount — even if more difficult — is the free action of individual wills, united in an ideal of progress for all.

Indeed, this ideal is outlined in the pages of his immortal "*Deche*"; but political adventurers and writers who court them will always find it easier — and cheaper — to read only "The Prince" and therefore to misunderstand Machiavelli.

2 Machiavelli, "*Deche,*" 1.4.

tour, who might have ranked with the statesmen of any European country. Admired abroad, revered by many in his own country, feared by all — what were the results of Diaz' régime, after thirty years of apparent peace and progress? This — that landowners and priests now pay the penalty of having enjoyed the advantages which his régime insured to them, without having spared a single thought to the assistance of a proletariat which they looked upon as born for slavery. The deepest impression I brought back from Mexico was that of the marks of century-old suffering engraved — despite years of victorious revolt — on the faces of Mexican village-dwellers. I always felt I was looking at the " wild beasts " as La Bruyère saw the French peasants, two generations before the Revolution.[3]

In the first chapter of this book I have already said how all Dictatorships eliminate the best from public

---

3 " *L'on voit certains animaux farouches, des mâles et des femelles, répandus par la campagne, livides et tout brûlés du soleil, attachés à la terre qu'ils fouillent et qu'ils remuent avec une opiniâtreté invincible; ils ont comme une voix articulée, et quand ils se lèvent sur leurs pieds, ils montrent une face humaine, et en effet ils sont des hommes. Ils se retirent la nuit dans des tanières, où ils vivent de pain noir, d'eau et de racines; ils épargnent aux autres hommes la peine de semer, de labourer et de recueillir pour vivre, et méritent ainsi de ne pas manquer de ce pain qu'ils ont semé.*"

Such were the words of La Bruyère. The reasons for the rapid bursting forth of the French Revolution are here.

And, 120 years later, so it was in Mexico.

office; the courageous servants, the critical minds, the creative brains.

If Porfirio Diaz was an exception to this rule, it was because he had not a bureaucracy to rely upon; Bismarck, who had one, killed all creative minds around him, and left nothing but *beamte* — officials.

Strange that all those who, following fashion's decree, hail dictators as saviors from the anonymous, unintelligent workings of modern bureaucracy, do not realize how bureaucracies are stronger under dictatorships than under any other régime. Their work is not checked by the Dictator, busied all day about his stage work; nor by Parliament, which has ceased to exist, under that régime, as a living force. In 1925, Mussolini was seriously ill for several months; during which time, the governmental machinery continued to work just as well or as badly as before. Even now, it may be said that the chief ruling organization in Italy is the Police, which has been inordinately increased by the Fascist régime, just as has happened in Russia.

This omnipotence of an anonymous bureaucratic administration, indirectly becomes an element of duration for a dictatorship — even on the psychological plane. Bureaucratic omnipotence, indeed, eliminates or suppresses all forms of local government, all possibility of political apprenticeship or political education. This, combined with the silence imposed on the Press, and the lack of public interest evinced for a mock-Parliament, cause timid folk to say:

— But, there is no possible successor . . .

No doubt, this question has always found an answer in history. It is nevertheless true that those towards whom people should have looked, in normal times, as to possible "successors," have either ruined themselves through compromise and cowardice, or they have been forgotten in the life of retirement and silence which they have been constrained to lead, or else they have been driven into exile.

Here is one of the reasons why the overthrow of dictatorships does not always bring an end to the evils they have brought about. To rule by fear, degrades ruler and ruled alike. Where the rulers live in fear, there they inspire fear. When for years the contact between rulers and ruled has been mainly through spies and eavesdroppers, the consequences can easily be foreseen. The mental prostration under dogmas, formulae, and men (exalted today by order, forgotten tomorrow by order, as happens all the time in Russia and Italy), is, in the long run, morally degrading. Such kinds of psychological evils risk becoming habits of thought, so deep-rooted as to remain after the causes have gone. The old Thucydides used to say: "The strength of a city is not ships or walls, but men."

He who has traveled in the ancient East has seen

243

races poisoned incurably by long generations of subjection to dictatorial despots.

This is the main reason why, even granted that a
" good Dictator " exists, what he effects will always
be lethal to a nation.

A study — as of a psychological phenomenon —
should be made of the many aspects and strange increase of collective cowardice in a country ruled by
dictatorship. The coward begins with a resigned
silence; but passes, by a process of gradual deteriora-
tion, to public demonstrations of enthusiasm for those
whom he still loathes from the bottom of his soul.
In course of time — who knows? — even this secret
feeling may disappear. Manzoni, who in his *Promessi
Sposi* has revived, in incomparable fashion, Italy of
the 17th century — that period of stifling Jesuit and
Spanish influence — has somewhere said: " When
men are forced to endure awful humiliations and in-
justice against which they cannot rebel, they end by
trying to forget their troubles, and to feel that their
position is not so horrible, after all; one step more,
and they do not even complain to their trustiest
friends. That would mean acknowledging what they
have sunk to. They prefer to forget." [4]

[4] And Chateaubriand, one of the rare Frenchmen who would
not bend to Bonaparte. even when the latter seemed to be lord of
Europe, wrote: " The whole country is become an empire of lies;
newspapers, speeches, prose and poetry, all distort the truth. If
it rains, we are assured that the sun is shining. Everything leads

THE FUTURE

In terminating these pages, where I tried to make the study of facts as serene as possible, it would be vain for me to hide that my thoughts run chiefly on the future of my own country, and the tasks whereto, as an Italian, I see her called for her honor's sake, for the sake of her mission in the world.

She will, naturally, long be reproached for having been the first to stumble into the Fascist adventure, and for having set the first example. This will be more injurious to her than the Second Empire was to France. Unjustly so; for if the first concrete staging for Fascism was Italy, the sickness it represents was a general sickness. Besides this, a day will come when what Bismarck said of the Second Empire protagonist will be repeated of the Italian one; " At a distance, it is something, but seen close to, it is nothing at all."

But Italians, free Italians, who never betrayed the

---

up to the Master alone. We must above all yell applause when a mistake or a crime has been committed. No book may appear without having pages in it given up to praise of him.

" The crimes of the Republican Revolution were the work of passions which always leave certain moral resources. But how heal the wound made by a government that has established despotism as a principle? which, talking the whole time of morality, is constantly destroying it? which mistakes a terrified condition of slavery for the calm of a well-organized society?

" The most terrible Revolutions are preferable to such a State."

traditions of Mazzini and Cavour, — Italians who have always carried their country in their hearts, like those seven thousand Israelites who alone refused to worship Baal — will some day be able to enjoy a bitter satisfaction. On the day of Mussolini's downfall, most commentators will at once begin to say that, after all, he was a noisy renegade from Socialism, a demagogue, a neurotic echo of the Kaiser's bombastic phrases.

In that day, the Italians who always denied him to be the possessor of any moral force, any constructive ideas, and who always saw through his performances, will be able to rise up and remind the world that those self-same critics — from New York to London and Paris — have for years past exuded admiration, eulogy, flattering comparisons. . . . And that moral complicity such as theirs had a share of responsiblity for what will have proved to be the duration of the Italian experiment.

But recriminations will only be a momentary luxury, when the dictatorial régimes are falling, one by one, in Europe. Products of a war neurosis, of that sudden loss of nerve which made so many countries tire of the slow, wearing toil through which — helped by no miracle — representative institutions are working, the immediate duty on that day of deliverance will be, to get back to that toil. Born of war, the Dictatorships have lived by war-time methods of propaganda. None of their successors will be able to profit by any of the incongruous ideas — syndicalist, nationalist, autocratic — which, borrowed from every quarter of the globe, were bound for an emblem into the lictor's bundle. In this — an Italian might feel tempted to say — Fascism will have done a service to the world's intellectual honesty. All its political masquerading will have done what the drunken slave did to Spartan youth.

If Fascism will have inflicted an injury on Italy which will take long to remove, an Italian who has never despaired of his country's future may well hope that she will draw from it fuller and deeper lessons than any other nation.

Those on whom will fall the painful task of succeeding to the Fascist adventure, will have a clear, stark duty before them, that no amount of bluff will be able to obscure.

Their belief in Liberty — as the sole way of a people's progress — will not for one moment make them forget the supreme necessity for safeguarding that without which society must dissolve: Justice, Order, Loyalty to the country; to safeguard them, above all, when they appear to be menaced: since hatred, even when excusable through years of suffering, may endanger justice; and the fictitious order maintained by the stifling influence of a Secret Police may teach men to forget the genuine, healthy order of countries

247

where all are free within the limits of the law; and loyalty to the country will be in danger of suffering from the blasphemous misuse of its sacred name, to which the interests of one faction have been putting it for many years.

From the steady carrying-out of these duties, even when they seem ungrateful tasks, those on whom will fall the responsibility of ruling countries hitherto subjected to Dictatorships, will draw the necessary moral strength and, the loyal support of the peoples who, to their cost, will have learnt the penalty of confiding one's destiny to demagogues.

When such a feeling of trust is everywhere awakened, the dangerous turning will be past.

For, with public evils, one part is always real and one part imaginary. I have seen this myself, when Poincaré came to power in France the last time. Financial panic, blind fright in the middle classes, and surly uncertainty in the working classes, all were present. Came Poincaré; he took no extraordinary measures, but governed honestly and inspired confidence; and the French recovered; but, as many of them had been looking for a miracle, they ascribed the merit to Poincaré, the thaumaturgist.

After all, we have been wrong to call the postwar Caesarean régimes, Dictatorships. The Roman Dictator represented a function of Republican Rome, not only in keeping with the idea of liberty, but constituting an actual proof — by the plenitude of his power, by its brief duration, and the supreme control of the Senate — that a reign of liberty may find the most varied solutions for the gravest problems and perils.

From this point of view, Cavour was a Dictator; Thiers, after the Bonapartist disaster of 1870, was another; Masaryck also, during the foundation of the Czechoslovakian State.

Poincaré, as I said before, was in his honest Republican way a Dictator too. The France of yesterday has seen two survivors of the Montagnards and Girondins, in Clemenceau and Poincaré. Clemenceau, the Jacobin, was completely at home when exercising absolute power. Poincaré, the Democrat, once success was attained, stole away from his deserved popularity — modestly attributing all credit to the Republic.

I have no doubt to which of these two history will ascribe the truer civic greatness.

When the day of reckoning of the present régimes has dawned, it will be in this spirit of liberty that the freed nations must accept those who will undertake the clearing-up of so much falsehood and error, and must grant them unusual powers, if they are to safeguard freedom against disorder and anarchy. For, if those who are so unselfish as to undertake the task are not endowed with all the power they need, every passion, delusion and egotism in the world will

249

swiftly be unchained, beyond immediate hope of restraint.

This danger past, the successors to Dictatorship should hasten to remove themselves, and account for everything they did.

Account for everything, I have said. Perhaps the whole problem of Democracy in the present world lies there.

Nothing is further from our thoughts, from us who, under Dictatorial rule, have never for an instant flinched in our fight for liberty, than to identify Democracy with parliamentary institutions, such as suited 19th century needs. In the first chapter I have said how, in my opinion, these could be brought into line with modern forms of social and economic life. Parliamentary institutions are a form of freedom. But the essential freedom, without which a people is doomed to decline, is freedom of thought, of speech, of the Press, of association. In the exercise of such freedom, we shall — once clear of the storm — find the solution of the Parliamentary problem. It would be easy to propose, now, at once, some attractive quack remedies, to convey the impression that the frame-work of future Democracy is ready-made in our minds; but, not being charlatans, we leave such performances to Dictators and would-be Dictators. I have, in the first chapter, stated my firm belief in decentralization, as a means of re-enhancing Parliamentary prestige; I'll simply add here, as an example, that (in my own opinion as well as that of eminent Italian friends of mine) even the central government ought to be decentralized; by which, I mean that we should welcome the creation of non-political, non-party councils attached to each State department, for the discussion of laws before these were submitted to Parliament, as well as regulations for the enforcing of laws. Thus, not only would the task of Parliament be considerably lightened, but the quality of the material it should work on would, technically at least, be greatly improved.

But all this belongs to the future. Only demagogues can dispose of miracle-working formulae. All we can say to the peoples, now, is that their salvation must be their own work.

As for Parliaments, proof has been made after a few years of Dictatorships. Parliaments of the first two decades of the 20th century everywhere showed signs of decadence; but their faults could at any rate be discussed and exposed; it was something. Then came Dictatorships, destroying Parliaments. All the faults of the latter went, redoubled, to form the Dictatorial mechanism — only, it became *tabu* to mention these faults, like the Dictators themselves.

It was the punishment of the Dictatorships which sank, and are still sinking, into an ever deepening slough of servility, corruption and intrigue such as could not exist under a Parliament, if only because the freedom to accuse and expose still existed.

The very experiment of Dictatorships has proved that not only are Liberalism and Democracy far from having accomplished their mission in the world; but that their work during the 19th century was but the beginning of a human liberation of which, by changing methods, they are still to be the instruments.

Liberalism and Democracy alone can rescue us from the new forms of slavery, which menace us through Russia and through the intellectual degradation that must be the final result of militarist and nationalist Dictatorships.

In one case only, it might be conceded that the future is not to Democracy; supposing it possible for the Western world to lapse once more into such a catastrophe of barbarism as precipitated itself, in the 4th and 5th centuries, upon Roman civilization.

But, granted such a thing to be impossible, we and our sons will see all the nations return to the ideals of Democracy, purified by the trials of blood-stained violence which has essayed to arrest progress. If, then, our sons will have learned that Liberty is a right which must be won anew each day, and which must be deserved, our trials will not have been in vain. In a world of crisis, the pure doctrine preached by Mazzini to our fathers, remains true: " You will not have things better, until you are better yourselves."

INDEX

INDEX

(Only names of the nineteenth and twentieth centuries have been included in this index. The addition of *n* indicates footnote.)

INDEX

256